Soil Salinity and Alkalinity

NIPA® GENX ELECTRONIC RESOURCES & SOLUTIONS P. LTD.
New Delhi-110 034

About the Author

Dr. Anandkumar Naorem, currently employed as a scientist at ICAR-Central Arid Zone Research Institute in Jodhpur, India, previously held the position of Head-in-charge at ICAR-CAZRI, RRS-Bhuj, India. He completed his bachelor's degree at Assam Agricultural University, Assam, India, and pursued his master's degree in soil microbiology and bioformulation at the College of Post-Graduate Studies, Central Agricultural University, Meghalaya, India. His doctoral research, conducted at Bidhan Chandra Krishi Viswavidyalaya in West Bengal, India, focused on the remediation of soil heavy metals for safer crop cultivation.

Dr. Naorem, who has authored several national and international publications, has received national recognition, including the 2015 Best Zonal Master's Thesis award from the Indian Society of Soil Science and the UGC-Maulana Azad National Fellowship for Minority Students (India). He is acknowledged for his contributions as a young scientist by numerous societies and organizations, having led various research projects on soil quality in arid regions, studies on elevated carbon dioxide levels, and investigations into halophytes. Notably, he has played a key role in international initiatives promoting spineless cactus as a dryland feed option in Gujarat.

---

for other volumes of
The Professional's Notes Series

The Professional's Notes Series
Volume 03
Soil Salinity and Alkalinity

Anandkumar Naorem
Scientist, Division of IFS
ICAR-Central Arid Zone Research Institute
Ministry of A&Fw, Government of India
Jodhpur-342003, Rajasthan, India

NIPA® GENX ELECTRONIC RESOURCES & SOLUTIONS P. LTD.
New Delhi-110 034

**NIPA® GENX ELECTRONIC
RESOURCES & SOLUTIONS P. LTD.**

101,103, Vikas Surya Plaza, CU Block
L.S.C.Market, Pitam Pura, New Delhi-110 034
Ph : +91 11 27341616, 27341717, 27341718
E-mail: newindiapublishingagency@gmail.com
www: www.nipabooks.com

For customer assistance, please contact
Phone: + 91-11-27 34 17 17
Fax: + 91-11- 27 34 16 16
E-Mail: feedbacks@nipabooks.com

Print ISBN: 978-93-58873-01-6

ebook ISBN: 978-93-58873-07-8

Composed and Designed by NIPA®.

Preface

In this third volume, we will identify the complex realm of problematic soils, examining the impacts of soil acidity, salinity, and alkalinity on soil quality, crop health, and soil biota. Problematic soils, characterized by high levels of acidity, salinity, or alkalinity, pose significant challenges to agricultural productivity, ecosystem sustainability, and land use management. Salt affected soils soils are often found in arid and semi-arid regions, where limited rainfall and high evaporation rates exacerbate the accumulation of salts and minerals in the soil profile. In addition, anthropogenic activities such as improper irrigation practices, excessive fertilizer application, and deforestation can contribute to soil degradation and the proliferation of problematic soils. Soil acidity, salinity, and alkalinity can have profound effects on soil quality, nutrient availability, and plant health. Acidic soils, characterized by low pH levels, can inhibit nutrient uptake by plants, leading to nutrient deficiencies and reduced crop yields. Saline soils, on the other hand, contain high levels of soluble salts, which can disrupt osmotic balance in plant cells, inhibit root growth, and cause physiological stress to crops. Alkaline soils, with high pH levels, can also impede nutrient availability and hinder plant growth, particularly for acid-loving crops.

Furthermore, these soil stresses not only affect crop health but also impact soil biota, including bacteria, fungi, protozoa, and nematodes. Soil organisms are highly sensitive to changes in soil chemistry and physical properties, and their abundance, diversity, and activity can be significantly impacted by soil acidity, salinity, and alkalinity. As a result, soil biota play a crucial role in mediating soil health and ecosystem function, and their resilience to soil stresses is essential for maintaining soil fertility and ecosystem resilience.

In this volume, we explore the mechanisms underlying soil acidity, salinity, and alkalinity, as well as their effects on soil quality, crop health, and soil biota. By understanding the complex interactions between soil chemistry, biology, and physics, we can develop strategies to mitigate the impacts of problematic soils and promote sustainable land management practices.

With gratitude and anticipation,

Anandkumar Naorem

Contents

Soil Salinity and alkalinity

In arid and semi-arid regions — not enough rainfall to leach - evaporation

- in humid areas too — deltaic regions — low lying areas also.
- major salts - Cl^-, SO_4^{2-}, CO_3^{2-}, HCO_3^{2-} of Ca, Mg and Na.
- solubility of CO_3^{2-} of Ca ($CaCO_3$) = 0.013 g/L; CO_3^{2-} of Mg ($MgCO_3$) = 2.5 g/L } low, ↑ with ↑ pCO_2 and ↓ pH
- But Cl^-, SO_4^{2-}, CO_3^{2-} of Na are high.

NaCl	Na_2SO_4	Na_2CO_3
264 g/L	162 g/L	178
nibir	label	lateg

- SO_4^{2-} of Ca = 1.9 g/L (low) ($CaSO_4$)
  Mg = 262 g/L (high) $MgSO_4$
- Cl^- of Ca and Mg : 7400 g/L at 20°C.

Extent of Problem

- 952 mha — world due to excessive salts (quosan) — FAO, UNESCO Map. 1974. (Mha) mrm → 343 (salinity); → 609 (alkalinity) badq
- Central Soil Salinity Research Institute, Karnal Haryana.
- In India — Total — 7421 thousand ha (turnel)
  - Gujarat 1649 (labourq) (2.20 Mha)
  - Rajasthan 1183 (lolgem) (1.37 Mha) ~~Gujarat~~ → Uttar Pradesh

Acc to 2010: 6.74 Mha — sodic 3.78; saline 2.96; — 0.37

- Elements in earth crust (%)

Oxygen	49 (raq) ← 46.5	Al	7 (t)
Si	26 (nib)	H	1 (l)
Ca	3 (m)	C	0.35
Na	2 (n)	Cl	0.20
Mg	2 (n)	S	0.10
K	2 (n)		

Common sources

- Rocks and minerals

Halite (NaCl)
Gypsum ($CaSO_4 \cdot 2H_2O$)
Sulphides (Pyrites, FeS_2)
Calcite ($CaCO_3$)
Dolomite [$CaMg(CO_3)_2$]
Apatite [$Ca_{10}(PO_4)_6F_2$]
Olivine [$(Mg, Fe)SiO_4$]
Feldspars → Albite ($NaAlSi_3O_8$)
→ Anorthite ($CaAl_2Si_2O_8$)
→ Orthoclase ($KAlSi_3O_8$)

- gradual release of salts due to geochemical, geohydrological proc. at exposed rocks and min.
- Salts originate - hydrolysis, hydration, carbonation, oxid-red.

Primary layer silicates
Biotite [$K(Mg, Fe, Mn)_3Si_3AlO_{10}(OH)_2$]
Glauconite [$K(Fe, Mg, Al)_2Si_3AlO_{10}(OH)_2$]

- From acid magmatic (eg. granite, gneiss)
salt coln ↳ CO_3^{2-}, SO_4^{2-}, Cl^-, silicates of Na.
alkaline magmatic (basalt, diabase)
↳ CO_3^{2-}, SO_4^{2-}, silicates of Ca, Mg

- Each molecular unit of Na-feldspar produces one mol. unit of $NaHCO_3$
Ca-feldspar - $Ca(HCO_3)_2$

Ocean H_2O
42×10^{15} tonnes of dissolved salts
↳ 85.6% NaCl.

- rain H_2O near sea coast → high concn of Cl^- of Na and Mg
inland rain H_2O → SO_4^{2-} and HCO_3^{-} of Ca and Mg

- Atmospheric accession of salts — falling dried droplets of ocean H_2O from atm along with rain or as dry salt dust
- Marine rock and evaporites
  - due to upliftment of many parts of continent
  - ↳ from sea/ocean — ppt — halides (NaCl), gypsum, sulphides (FeS_2) } dominant soluble salt
  - some are ppt; some remain trap in alluvium
- Salt springs — volcanic gases and H_2O from interior — large quantities of Cl^-
- Economic activities — irrigation without adequate drainage.
  - flooding by H_2O from mining shafts or ind. effluents.

Origin of salt-affected (5)

↳ Continental cycles — movement, redistribution, acc^m of CO_3^{2-}, SO_4^{2-}, Cl^- in inland regions.

↳ Marine — acc^m of NaCl from ocean in lowlands of coastal

↳ Deltaic — mov & acc of salts carried by rivers from continents or delta valley

↳ Artesian — acc. of salts due to evap. of deep ground H_2O or ground streams (wedged up to surface through tectonic features or other processes.)

↳ Anthropogenic - salt acc. due to erroneous human a.

- Highly leachable salts — NaCl, Na_2SO_4, Na_2CO_3, $NaHCO_3$, $MgCl_2$, $MgSO_4$, $CaCl_2$ — (Cl^-, SO_4^{2-})

- Salt Water Balance = controls salt acc^m process.
- for high land internally well-drained

$$D_{rw} \cdot C_{rw} + D_{iw} \cdot C_{iw} = D_{ew} \cdot C_{ew} + D_{dw} \cdot C_{dw} \pm S$$

(S = change in salt content)

D = depth
C = salt conc^n

rw = rain water
iw = irrigation H_2O
ew = water evapotranspired
dw = drainage or percolating H_2O

| no H_2O rising due to capillary action

- for low lying areas

$$D_{rw} \cdot C_{rw} + D_{iw} \cdot C_{iw} + D_{cw} \cdot C_{cw} = D_{dw} \cdot C_{dw} + D_{ew} C_{ew} \pm S$$

| H_2O rising due to capillary action.

cw = capillary action.

C_{rw}
D_{sw} } negligible = practical value = 0.
C_{ew}

When inputs > outputs – salt accumulation
evaporation > rainfall – ,,

- Salinization doesn't occur – deep water table (>10 m) despite dryness

CHARACTE. OF SALT AFF. SOILS.

- Total salt concentration – EC or ECe (Electrical conductance)

Sum of all major soluble cations = anions [mmol/L]

↳ milli mhos/cm at 25°C
deci siemens/m
1 S = 1 mho (SI unit)
1 dS/m = 1 mmho/cm

pH [1:2 soil : H_2O suspension] & sat. paste
EC [1:2 ,, ,,]
soluble cations
,, anions
exc. cations
exch. Na Perc.
CEC, $CaCO_3$ content

- For soils EC 0.1 – 5 dS/m.

TDS (mg/L) = EC (dS/m) × 640

Sum of soluble cations or anions (mmol/L) = EC (dS/m) × 10

- For soils EC 3 – 30 dS/m.

OP (bars) = EC (dS/m) × (–0.36)

↳ osmotic potential / –ve osmotic pressure of solution.
↓
measures effect of salinity on plant growth.

- Why EC?

Saturation percentage (SP) ∝ plant-available moisture range i.e. PWP – FC.

Moisture content at PWP = ½ of FC
¼ of SP

∴ Soluble salt concn in saturation extract = ½ of concn at FC.
= ¼ at PWP.

↓

Reason why EC_e can be used for appraising effects of soil salinity on plant growth.

lag sir

- Exchangeable Sodium Percentage (ESP)
- Sodium Adsorption ratio (SAR)

} US Salinity lab, 1954.

$$ESP = 100 \times \frac{(\text{Exchangeable } Na^+ \text{ ions})}{CEC}$$

⇒ mmol (+) / kg of soil.
= 0.1 meq / 100 g soil.

$$SAR = \frac{[Na^+]}{\sqrt{\frac{[Ca^{2+} + Mg^{2+}]}{2}}}$$ > mmol/L

↳ 2 outside the square root

⇒ ESR / ~~ESP~~ = $K_G \cdot SAR$

↳ Gapon constant (values from 0.01 – 0.015)

$$ESR = \frac{X_{Na}}{X_{Ca} + X_{Mg}}$$ X = exchangeable (X) cations mmol/kg soil.

$\frac{ESP}{100}$ = ESR = for irrigated soils ESP < 25 – 30

$$ESP = \frac{100\ ESR}{1 + ESR}$$

assuming $CEC = X_{Na^+} + X_{Ca^{2+}} + X_{Mg^{2+}}$

Classification of Salt-affected Soils

1954 US Salinity Laboratory → saline / saline-alkali / alkali.

But – on basis of kinds of salts on properties of these soils and plant growth → saline / alkali

Saline

- Cl^-, SO_4^{2-} of Na, Ca, Mg
  neutral salts

Refer Ext.

- characterized by saline ~~efflor~~ efflorescence or white encrustation
- called as reh and thur.

- presence of gypsum
- pH of saturation paste (pHs) < 8.5

  ESP < 15

  $EC_e > 4$ dS/m at 25°C.

- Cl^-, SO_4^{2-} of Na, Ca, Mg
- Ratio $\frac{[Na^+]}{[Cl^-]+[SO_4^{2-}]} < 1$
- dominance of Ca, Mg
- flocculation
- divalent (Ca^{2+}) ion → ↓ zeta potential (ξ) of soil exchange complex → attraction of clay particles.
- $Al^{3+} > Ca^{2+} > Mg^{2+} > K^+ > Na^+$ → reverse in dispersion.

Alkali soils

- sodium saturation
- CO_3^{2-} and HCO_3^{2-} of Na
- absence of gypsum unlike saline soils. Refer txt (sparingly soluble)
- Usar and Kallar

  pH > 8.5

  ESP > 15

  EC < 4 ds/m.

- Ratio $\frac{[Na^+]}{[Cl^-]+[SO_4^{2-}]} > 1$
- when om dispersed — alkali soils — dark brown black appearance

Alkalinity of alkali soils

$$Alk = [HCO_3^-] + 2[CO_3^{2-}]$$

$$Alk = [Na^+] + [K^+] + 2[Ca^{2+}] + 2[Mg^{2+}] - [Cl^-] - 2[SO_4^{2-}]$$

$$pH = \log Alk - \log P_{CO_2} + 7.82$$

10 fold change in alkalinity or 10-time change in P_{CO_2} → unit change in pH.

- alkalinity depends on
  - relative concn of Na_2CO_3
  - $NaHCO_3$
  - partial pressure of CO_2

Formation of carbonates for Na and alkalisation

- as a result of carbonation of alumino-silicate minerals in presence of H_2O

$NaAlSi_3O_8 + H_2O + CO_2 \longrightarrow HAlSi_3O_8 + NaHCO_3$

Albite

$\hookrightarrow + 7OH \longrightarrow Al(OH)_3$ (Gibbsite) $+ 3Si(OH)_4$ (soluble silica)

$2NaHCO_3 \longrightarrow Na_2CO_3 + CO_2 + H_2O$

↳ highly soluble

↳ hydrolysis results in high alkalinity (pH ↑ upto 12)

$Na_2CO_3 + 2H_2O \longrightarrow 2Na^+ + 2OH^- + H_2CO_3$

In presence of CO_2 → pH ↓ → because formation of $NaHCO_3$.

$Na_2CO_3 + H_2O + CO_2 \longrightarrow 2NaHCO_3$.

- release of CO_2 from decomposition of OM → accentuates prodn of $NaHCO_3$ formation → excessive evaporation → double salt crystals ($Na_2CO_3 \cdot NaHCO_3 \cdot 2H_2O$).

→ relative proportion of Na^+ w.r.t Ca^{2+} and Mg^{2+} → ↑

→ $Ca\text{-}X + 2Na^+_s \rightleftharpoons 2Na\text{-}X + Ca_s^{2+} \longrightarrow$ ESP ↑. Reason:- with ↑ evapot. ↓ ↑ concn of soil soln. $CaSO_4$, $CaCO_3$, $MgCO_3$ — concn ↑ → ppt

X = soil exchange sites

S = solution.

→ In most arid and semi-arid, → contain $CaCO_3$ → constant Hydrolysis of $CaCO_3$ produces OH^- → OH^- in maintaining higher pH in calcareous alkali soils than in non-cal. alk.

- dispersion. - dispersed clay part move down — compact layer.

- ↑ zeta potential (highly hydrated Na^+ ions)

→ ↓ HC. → irrigation H_2O stagnates at the surface.

- very hard and dry and sticky when wet.

Saline-alkali soils

- ECe > 4 dS/m at 25°C
- ~~pH > 8.5~~ | formed as a result both of salinization & alka.
- ESP > 15
- when EC ↑ → ↑ concn due to Cl^- and SO_4^{2-} of Na^+ so, → pH < 8.5
- clay - flocculated
- when ECe ↓ due to soluble CO_3^{2-} of Na → pH → pH > 8.5
- with leaching of soluble salts of Cl^- & SO_4^{2-} of Na → behaves like alkali soils.

Refer for the rest to NB

Taxonomy (Soil Survey Staff, 1975).

- Order - Aridisol (optional Alfisol, Mollisol, Inceptisol, Vertisol)

having calcic, gypsic, salic, natric | high EC | absence of mollic, oxic, spodic

Effects on plant growth

- seedling germination
- foliage bluish green
  - cells divide but not elongate
  - ↑ no. of cells per unit area.
- semi-permeable membrane of roots - passes H_2O not salts → so stress in H_2O uptake
- so need efficient irrigation
- ability of the plants → produce organic a... or uptake of salts → osmotically adjust
- necrosis, burning of leaf tips and margins - death.
- But - some plants - selective absorption mechanism.
- Excessive alkalinity - caustic effect on roots

- Nutritional imbalances.
  excessive absorption of Na^+ → reduce abso. of Ca^{2+}, Mg^{2+}, K^+

  ↑ HCO_3^{2-} → ↓ Fe → Fe chlorosis (↳ e[illegible])

  ↑ pH → deficiency of micronutrients cations
- affect soil biology, mineralization of OM and transformation of applied fertilizer.

- Relative salt tolerance

- Threshold level
- relative growth at soil salinity levels exceeding threshold levels of a crop — estimated using response function.

  ↓

  Two linear lines

  i) zero slope → yield stability under ↑ levels of salinity

  ii) growth ↓ → ↑ levels of salinity →

  $$Yr = 100\,b\,(EC_e - a)$$

  Yr = yield

  a = threshold salinity dS/m

  b = slope expressed in % per dS/m

- sodicity tolerant crops – karnal grass, rhodes grass, para grass.
- Most sensitive stages – germination, and early seedling establishment
  - change from vegetative to reproductive phase

Management

- adequate drainage.
- leaching
- replacement of Na^+

Threshold salinity

Rice - 3 dS/m

Wheat - 6 dS/m

Maize - 1.7 dS/m

- Drainage system principle: water flows in direction of maxm decrease of hydraulic head and flow velocity ∝ to hydraulic gradient.
- dispersion and flocculation → cations in soil solution and those adsorbed.

Physical Amelioration

- deep ploughing }
- sub-soiling } break the impermeable layer
- sanding — change the texture
- profile inversion - when surface soil is good
- scrapping - most farmers do it, but not permanent

Hydro-technical Amelioration

- Removal of salts from saline soil
- Replacement of Na^+ ions from the exchange complex of alkali soils. through leaching and drainage.

- Extent of leaching depends on —

a) soil properties
b) initial salinity and chemical comp. of salts
c) quality of H_2O
d) leaching methods.
e) water-table depth.
f) efficiency of drainage system
g) salt tolerance of the crop.

- leaching efficiency = $\frac{\text{quantity of salts removed per unit}}{\text{depth of water}}$

- Leaching Requirement = $\frac{Ddw}{Diw} = \frac{Ciw}{Cdw}$ (for upland)

$= \frac{Ddw}{Diw}$.

- with increase ~~of~~ in salinity of irrigation H_2O, more water (Ddw) will have to be applied
- Leaching Fraction (LF) = fraction of depth of applied irrigation H_2O that leaves root zone as drainage H_2O.

Leaching Methods

- Ponding continuously or intermittently
- Land levelling imp. before leaching
- As a rule, leaching should be done with depth of H_2O = depth of soil to be reclaimed.
- Passage of 1 m leaching water per 1 m of soil depth under continuous pond — removes approx. 80% of soluble salts
- Basin furrow method — needs less water

Drainage

- in shallow water table — sub-soil drainage — but more expensive

Chemical Amelioration

Amendments → directly or indirectly mobilize divalent cations for replacement of sodium f. b leaching

- Sources
  - soluble sources of Ca. (Gypsum, $CaCl_2$, phospho-gypsum)
  - Sparingly soluble Ca salts (Calcite)
  - Acids or acid formers (S, H_2SO_4, SO_4^{2-} of Fe and Al, pyrites, lime-sulphur)

- Presence of alkaline earth carbonates $CaCO_3$ → acids/acid formers used.

- non-calcareous — acids not recommended.

Gypsum

$2Na\text{-}X + CaSO_4 \rightleftharpoons Ca\text{-}X + Na_2SO_4$

$CaCl_2$

$2Na\text{-}X + CaCl_2 \rightleftharpoons Ca\text{-}X + 2NaCl$

S

$2S + 3O_2 \rightarrow 2SO_3$

$SO_3 + H_2O = H_2SO_4$

$H_2SO_4 + CaCO_3 \rightarrow CaSO_4 + Ca(HCO_3)_2$

$2Na\text{-}X + CaSO_4 \rightleftharpoons Ca\text{-}X + Na_2SO_4$

- microbial oxidation of Sulphur – aerobic Thiobacilli – chemoautotrophs.

Pyrites → formation of H_2SO_4

$2FeS_2 + 7O_2 + 2H_2O = 2FeSO_4 + 2H_2SO_4$

$2CaCO_3 + H_2SO_4 \rightarrow CaSO_4 + Ca(HCO_3)_2$

$2Na\text{-}X + CaSO_4 \rightleftharpoons Ca\text{-}X + Na_2SO_4$

- $CaCl_2$ is highly soluble but hygros. and costly
- gypsum mostly recommended
- Calibrating a sodic soil with gypsum soln of known Ca concn and then estimate Ca deficit.

$GR\ (cmol/kg\ soil) = (E_{Nai} - E_{Naf})\ CEC$

↓ initial exc. Na. ↓ final

for, per ha

$GR\ (kg/ha) = 1720 \times (E_{Nai} - E_{Naf})\ CEC.$

- To compensate lack of a quantitative replacement –
  GR × 1.25
- Gypsum – broadcast or incorporated
  but mixing in deeper soil ↓ its effectiveness → gypsum
  react with soluble carbonates to ppt Ca as $CaCO_3$.

ESP range

60 - 70 — Rice

30 – 50 — wheat

Biological Amelioration

- OM and action of plant roots
- Rice – preferred to grown during reclamation process of alkali – ponding – build up of pCO_2 → leaching of salts
- ↳ first depletion of O → ↑ pCO_2 (more in organic)
  ↓
  solubilize native $CaCO_3$ and release
  Ca removes Na →
  → ↑ pCO_2 → ↑ reduction in pH and ESP of soil

→ Na → intensifies soil reduction (how)
  ↳ dispersion ↗

Soil Air and Temperature

SOIL ACIDITY

- Dissociation constant of water

$$k_w = [H^+][OH^-]$$
$$= [10^{-7}][10^{-7}]$$
$$= 10^{-14} \text{ at } 25°C.$$

$pH = \log \frac{1}{[H^+]}$

$= -\log[H^+]$

= measures H^+ activity (Activity = Concn × Act. coefficient)

= logarithmic expression

↳ each unit change in pH → 10-fold change in acidity or basicity

- Danish chemist Sorenson in 1909. (S.P.L. Sorenson)

- Soil pH measures $[H^+]$ in soil solution only (active acidity)

Sources of soil acidity

- Exc. H^+ and Al^{3+} → mainly responsible
- Fe and Al oxides
- Soil OM
- clay minerals.

Active acidity → H^+ ions in soln.

Potential acidity → H^+ ions in various chemical combination

- and adsorbed on surfaces of solid part.

H^+ → permanent charge on mineral surfaces because exc. H^+ in soil neutralize charge arising from

→ isomorphous substitution of cations

pH-dependent charge may arise from structural OH^- groups at corners/edges of clay.

↳ which dissociate into H^+.

t $pH < 5.0$, Al^{3+} becomes soluble → adsorbed by silicate clays or bound by OM → Al^{3+} then hydrolysed in soil soln releasing H^+ ions → soil acidity

$$Al^{3+} + 2H_2O \rightleftharpoons Al(OH)_2^+ + 2H^+$$

Thus, in strongly acidic → H^+ activity in soil soln is very high

So, adsorbed H^+ → lesser magnitude in strongly acidic.

- In moderately acidic — Bulk of Al^{3+} convert to → Al. hydroxy ions.
  ↓ some are adsorbed and ad as ex. ions.
  - remain equilm with soln

$$Al^{3+} + OH^- \longrightarrow Al(OH)^{2+}$$

$$Al(OH)^{2+} + OH^- \longrightarrow Al(OH)_2^+$$

- In soln → hydrolyse and produce H^+

$$Al(OH)^{2+} + H_2O \rightarrow Al(OH)_2^+ + H^+$$

$$Al(OH)_2^+ + H_2O \longrightarrow Al(OH)_3 + H^+$$

pH	$[H^+]$
1	$= 10^{-1}$ mol/L
2	$= 10^{-2}$ mol/L

- At $pH < 5$ → Fe behaves like Al → but acidity is much less.
- In acid sulphate soils — Kuttanad area of Kerala and Sunderbans of WB → dissolved or free acidic substances — H_2SO_4 or $Al_2(SO_4)_3$, $Fe_2(SO_4)_3$ cause acidity
- At $pH > 5$ → amorphous Al and Fe hydroxyl complexes → hydrolysis ↓ contribute H^+.
- Fine textured soils with ↑ OM → more H^+ ions.
- High Al^{3+} concn in root — disturb P uptake
- " " " inside cell — disturb sugar phosphorylation
- SOM — carboxylic and phenolic groups — weak acids — dissociate → H^+.

Classification of soil acidity

- ↳ active — soln (H^+ or Al^{3+} in solution) — small fraction - but imp — since plant roots and microbes around rhizosphere influenced by it — only small amt of lime needed
- ↳ pot exchangeable — in strongly acidic - adso. H^+ and Al^{3+} on colloids.
- ↳ reserve — Al. hydroxy ions, Al^{3+} and H^+ → non-exchangeable form with OM and clays.

Reserve acidity measured by

- titrating soil suspension upto a certain pH being (normally pH 8).
equivalent to amount of NaOH used.

- when acid soil → limed – gibbsite is formed from $Al(OH)_2^+$
with increase in pH

→ Potential acidity > active acidity
↳ more doses of lime needed. (so, no attempt to neutralize reserve acid).

- Liming – neutralize active acidity and part of exc. acidity.

Active and Potential acidity

- equilm between act & pot.
- Most important – CEC of exchange complex satisfied by bases.
- other factors: nature of clay or organic colloids.
  - kinds of adsorbed bases
  - concn of soluble salts in soil solution

$$\% \text{ base saturation} = \frac{\text{Exc bases (cmol/kg)}}{\text{CEC (cmol/kg)}} \times 100$$

- % base saturation < 50%, pH around 5.5 → acidity
- . . . . . 80% pH . . . 6.5 → neutral

Buffering of soil

- tolerance to change in pH of a solution | rise in pH is minimal until enough lime applied.
- rapid lowering of pH – prevented
↳ organic matter decomp – organic ac → ↑ temporary H^+ concn.

- H^+ and Al^{3+} along with adsorbed bases – control
- more clay and OM → ↑ BF
- higher CEC → ↑ BF
- degree of BF highest pH 4.5–6.0.
drops < 4.5, > 6.0.

- Soils ↑ in OM and clay (esp mont) /verm – high BC.

- Soils - same base satu. → highest pH - hydrous O of ~~Fe and clay mn~~.
- low pH - Al^{3+} and $Al(OH)_2^+$ react - block exchange sites in silicate clays and humus → ↓ CEC → lowest in 2:1 alum. clay
- So, liming → ↑ CEC → more Ca^{2+}, Mg^{2+} etc adsorbed. → So, for rise pH ↳ addn lime reqd.
- BF - due to weak acids and their salts
- CO_3^{2-}, HCO_3^{2-} and PO_4^{3-} → buff. agents. pH intermediate kaolinite & humus.
- Organic a - due to microb. activity - weak acids.

BC → due to potential H^+ of exchange complex and its ass. cations.

Soil reaction correlations

- nitrification slow < 5.5
- Under acid - pH dependent NH_4^+ fixation ↓ with ↓ pH
- At low pH, Fe, Al, Mn - soluble - toxic
  high pH - deficient
- $H_2PO_4^-$, HPO_4^{2-} → pH dependent → mostly available in neutral or slightly acidic
  ↳ ↓ as strongly acidic/alkaline.
- → Micronutrient cations - ↑ acidity ↑.
  anions → ↓. in acidity ↑ (Mo, B)
- effect of soil acidity on leguminous crops - due to Mo deficiency rather than Al toxicity
- In acid organic - Cu deficient but not in acid mineral soil.
- Bac. and actino. → mild acidic, neutral, high pH
  fungi → acidic
- → Rhizobium - less effective in acidic
- pH 6.0 - 7.2 - most suitable for crops.
- Fe reqd of rhododendrons → ↑.
- → Forest trees can tolerate acidity

Acid - forming factors

- acidic parent material - granite
- leaching of bases - heavy ppt - formation of $CaSO_4$ → leachable.
- Use of acidic fert. - $(NH_4)_2SO_4$, NH_4NO_3 → form $CaSO_4$ → leachable
- stronger organic a ↳ microbial decay - carbonic a → solvent action remove base forms cations like Ca, Mg.

- Inorganic acids – H_2SO_4, HNO_3.
- Rain H_2O pH 5.6 – due to presence of carbonic a.
  Rait under influence of burning fossil fuels or smelting – low as 4.0

Determination of soil pH — pH meter

- Jackson, 1973, pH meter — glass electrode — Haber and Klemsiewicz 1909
- Two electrodes – placed in soil suspension in water
- one is glass electrode which measures activity of H^+ ions.
- Two electrodes
  ↳ Glass electrode – consists of thin bulb of glass separating soil suspen. from an acid solution (HCl) of known H^+ ion, immersed an internal ref. electrode of AgCl / Cl^- or $HgCl_2/Cl^-$.
- Electrometric potential developed across glass membrane
- Another electrode – external reference electrode (calomel electrode) – KCl soln. Hg covered with (calomel) $HgCl_2$

Electrochemical cell:

$$Hg, Hg_2Cl_2, KCl \parallel H^+_{(a_1)} \vdots H^+_{(a_2)} \parallel KCl, Hg_2Cl_2, Hg$$

$$Eemf\ (E) = E_{ref} + \frac{2.303\ RT}{F}\ pH$$

$$pH = \frac{E - E_{ref}}{2.303\ RT} = \frac{E - E_{ref}}{0.059} \text{ at } 25°C$$

E_{ref} = emf of external reference electrode.

- pH value of soil soln decreases through diffused layer close to –vely charged surface
- pH is measured in soil suspension or in paste
- pH 0.2–0.5 unit lower.
  ↳ Ca – flocculation minimise paste and dilution effect –
- pH of a soil having 0.01 M $CaCl_2$ – unaffected (Based on Ratio law).
- Ca – most abundant basic metal cation –
  addn of $CaCl_2$ → don't change proportn. of ex. cations and measurement of pH in 0.01 M $CaCl_2$ – advantageous.

- It compresses diffuse layer and suppresses hydrolysis.
- 1:1 soil/water pastes → pH one unit or more lower than a 1:5 soil/water suspension.
- Also Soil: water ratio, electrolyte content and CO_2 – affect pH
- Soils pH >8.5 and contain free Na_2CO_3 and other soluble salts – show increase in pH when soil : water ratio is high

↓

Dilution ↑ hydrolysis of sodium clay

↓

formation of NaOH

↓

pH ↑.

- So, 1:2.5 soil : water ratio is choosen.
- Ratio law.

$$\frac{[H^+]}{\sqrt{[Ca^{2+}]}} = pH - \frac{1}{2}pCa = \text{constant}$$

↓ Lime potential

- Value of LP dsn't depend on soil : H_2O ratio or salt content, measurement of pH in dilute aq. $CaCl_2$ is more dependable.
- Since pH and pCa – measured in clear solution – suspension effect avoided.
- By ↑ salt concn in alkaline soil → pH ↓ due to reduction of hydrolysis of ex. cations like Na^+.
- Genesis, Occurence, Characteristics
- leaching through parent acidic rock, heavy ppt accel. = main cause.

  - main cause = leaching of bases through parent acidic rock
  - In humid – heavy ppt acceler.
  - Mean annual temp, veg, parent rock, hydrolog. cond.

- In India – acc. drastic weathering – hot humid climate – heavy rainfall. under marshy cond.
- Laterization, Podzolization and accm of undec. OM – acidity
- 35% of Indian soil – strong to moderate
  65% – slightly acidic

  } 90% 90 Mha = 1/4 of total geog. area

- Base unsaturation within pH 5.0 - 6 - 16% - 67%

- NE acid soils → exch. Al^{3+}.
  - Extra Refer NB

Strong	pH<4.5	= 6
Moderate	4.5-5.5	= 25
Slightly	5.5-6.5	= 59
Total		- 90 Mha

Liming materials

Agricultural lime - Carbonates, oxides, hydroxides } of Ca, Mg

- Others are marl, oyster shells, industrial waste eg. slag.
- Burnt lime - oxide of lime / quick lime.
  ↳ more faster reaction in soil.

$CaCO_3 + Heat \rightarrow CaO + CO_2\uparrow$

$[CaMg(CO_3)_2] + Heat \rightarrow CaO + MgO + 2CO_2\uparrow$

- Add^n of H_2O to burnt lime — hydrated lime (slaked lime)
  - more caustic than burnt

$CaO + H_2O \rightarrow Ca(OH)_2$

$MgO + H_2O \rightarrow Mg(OH)_2$

| - economic lime mat.

Reactions of lime with CO_2 and colloids

- Lime + CO_2 + H_2O → bicarbonate

$CaO + H_2O + 2CO_2 \rightarrow Ca(HCO_3)_2$

$Ca(OH)_2 + 2CO_2 \rightarrow Ca(HCO_3)_2$

$CaCO_3 + H_2O + CO_2 \rightarrow Ca(HCO_3)_2$

- When lime reacts with soil colloids — replace H and Al^{3+} from colloidal phase.

$$\begin{matrix} H^+ \\ H^+ \end{matrix} \rangle clay + Ca(OH)_2 = Ca^{2+}\text{-}Clay + 2H_2O$$

$$\begin{matrix} H^+ \\ H^+ \end{matrix} \rangle clay + Ca(HCO_3)_2 = Ca^{2+}\text{-}Clay + 2H_2O + 2CO_2$$

Lime Requirement (factors affecting Lime req.).

→ buffer capacity.

reqd change in pH

→ chemical comp. of liming mat

→ fineness of liming.

- fine texture – more lime
- Calcitic or dolomitic – more slowly reacts than burnt lime and hydrated lime

Chemical Equivalence

- One mol. of CaO, MgO or $Ca(OH)_2$ – neutralizes the same amt of acidity – as one mol. of $CaCO_3$.
- $CaCO_3$ equivalent of burnt lime –

$$\frac{\text{mol wt of } CaCO_3}{\text{" } CaO} = \frac{106}{56} = 1.786 \times 100 = 178.6.$$

If burnt lime has 90% purity then 100 kg of it will have $CaCO_3$ equivalent of $90 \times 1.786 = 160.7$

- $CaCO_3$ equivalence of $MgCO_3$ = $\frac{CaO}{MgCO_3}$ = 0.67

Fineness of Liming Materials

- Liming factor → actual amt of lime read is calculated from estimated
  → 1.5 – 2 generally used.

10 mesh (10 wires/inch)
→ 2 mm
60 mesh — 0.25
200 — 0.075 mm
coarse part.

Refer NB

Measurement of Lime Requirement

- Exc. Al^{3+} as Lime Reqd-Index
  Al-toxicity pH < 5.0.
- Exc. Al^{3+} extracted by neutral unbufferred 1 N KCl soln
  → index of LR.

- Such index → soils of low CEC.

For high Al-tolerant

LR = 1 × Exc. Al.

medium

LR = 1.5 × Exc. Al.

~~high~~ low

LR = 2 × Exc. Al.

- Lime requirement = SMP
  = Shoemaker, Mcclean, Pratt

↓

- 5 ml DW + 10 ml of extractant buffer — pH 7.5
  - 1.8 g nitrophenol
  - 2.5 ml triethanolamine
  - 3 g K_2CrO_3
  - 2 g Ca-acetate
  - 53.2 g $CaCl_2 \cdot 2H_2O$

↓

5 g of soil

↓

stirred

↓

pH determined.

- SMP buffer method - based on relationship between buffer indicated lime-reqd and $CaCO_3$ incubation measured LR.

- SMP - soils with ↑ exc. Al^{3+} and high LR.

BaCl₂ - Triethanolamine method

- Mehlich
- $BaCl_2$-TEA buffer (pH 8)
- titrate fresh sample of buffer with acid down to measure pH of soil + buffer.

Diff between two titration = LR.

Management

- Minor millet (*Panicum miliare*)
- Finger " (*Eleusine coracana*)

- Gypsum - sub-soil acidity
  - ↳ Ca ↓ much down faster than lime.
  - -doesn't raise pH and CEC

  SO_4^{2-} anion released from Gyp. dissolution -accompanies Ca → Gyp. ↑ level of Ca and reduce ↓ Al.

- Indian slag — 1-7% P_2O_5

  25-50% CaO

  2-10% MgO

POTASSIUM

- biggest, among mineral cations – in non-hydrated size (0.1333 nm)
  with 8 or 12 no. of O_2 atoms surrounding.
- K-O bond weak.
- K-polarity = 0.088 nm^3 > Ca^{2+}, Mg^{2+}, Li^+ and Na^+
  < Ba^{2+}, Cs^{2+}, NH_4^+ and Rb^+.
  ↓
- high polarizability – preferred in ion-exchange
- hydration energy of 142.5 kJ g^{-1} ion^{-1}
  ↳ ↳ little ability to cause swelling.
  heat released when new bonds are made between ion and H_2O
- In plant cell sap- 100–200 mM
- not in organic compounds – but K^+ in solution in cell
- mobile in plants
- reqd for activation of 80 enzymes.

Deficiency Symptoms

- doesn't manifest immediately
- growth rate decreases – symptoms appear
- tips and margins of older leaves – yellow (chlorosis) – then die (necrosis).
- In forage and legume – white necrotic spots
  – mistaken as insect attack.

- slow and stunted growth
- weak stalks and susceptibility to lodging, pests and diseases. frost
- low yield
- poor quality of produce
- seeds- small, shrivelled
- fruit – low sugar – lack normal colouration
- Veget - Short shelf life. an

Potassium uptake and Requirement

- absorbed mostly during early growth stage
- Maize- 70-80% silking
  100% - 3-4 weeks after silking
- Po K in normal leaves- 1 to 4%
- Banana, pineapple, papaya, alfalfa, sugarcane - heavy feeders of K
- N, P ↑ → accelerate K uptake

K Minerals

- mostly dioctahedral micas
  - muscovite $KAl_3Si_3O_{10}(OH)_2$
  - gluconite
  - illite (hydrous mica)
- and trioctahedral micas
  - phlogopite $KMg_3AlSi_3O_{10}(OH)_2$
  - biotite $KAl(Mg,Fe)_3Si_3O_{10}(OH)_2$
  - feldspars
    - sanidine $(KAlSi_3O_8)$
    - orthoclase $(K, Na)AlSi_3O_8)$
    - microcline $(Na,K)AlSi_3O_8$
- also allophones ($2SiO_2 \cdot Al_2O_3 \cdot 3H_2O$ or $SiO_2 \cdot Al_2O_3 \cdot 2H_2O$) } - approx 1%
- 90-98% of K in soil - primary minerals - micas (biotite & musco)
  - K feldspar (orthoclase and microclane)
  - second minerals.
- Micas - Biotite weather ↑ than feldsp. → release K readily
- from non-exchangeable - slowly available - readily available

K Pools

Soil solution K — 0.1-0.2%
Exc. K (soil colloids) — 1-2%
non-exch (secondary min) — 1-10% or fixed
Structural K (primary min) — 90-98%

→ Exch K - more in black cotton and vertic type
→ non-exch - illite dominant alluvial soil.

- Ammonium acetate extractable

Equilibrium

solution, exchangeable → readily available

Factors affecting availability of K (6) TDCPLF

→ soil texture – fine texture ↑ (both avail & non-exch) — because of K bearing minerals in finer fraction of illite

more conspicuous in alluvial (illite) than in black (smectite) or red (kaolinite)

→ Clay Mineralogy – available K is high in smectite dominant

Vertisols f.b mixed mineralogy, illite and kaolonite) may have low amt of water soluble K compared to illite.

non-exchangeable } → high in micaceous minerals like illite
total K

- kaolinite – (laterite and red) – poor avail. K.

- Soil depth – ↓ with ↑ in depth → Calcareous alluvial (both avai & non-exch)

available K → surface
non-exc → sub-surface } alluvial soils of Indo-Gangetic Plains

In swell-shrink soil, both ↓ with ↑ depth.

- Soil pH

In low pH – H^+ and $Al(OH)_2^+$ compete – keep more K^+ in solution phase
– reduce fixation

pH increases – H^+ and $Al(OH)_2^+$ neutralize – fixation

So, K-availability → acid soils.

- Liming

↳ ↑ CEC → K adsorption ↑ → K in solution ↓

- (Freezing and Thawing) and Wetting and Drying

↳ release K from illite dominant
↳ no release from low quan of exch. K.

- drying – fixation ↑ → K decrease – esp. when exch K is ↑.

Quantity- Intensity Relationships

- Beckett (1964) (laqbour) and Tinker (1964) | Iqbr laqbour
- K supplying power
- Intensity — K in soil solution — immediately available (I)
- Quantity - replenishing capacity (Q)
- adsorption of K^+ influenced by Ca^{2+} and Mg^{2+} in soil solution
    - ↳ K activity ratio (AR_K) - instead of K concn alone to indicate INTENSITY FACTOR

$$AR_K = \frac{[K^+]}{\sqrt{[Ca^{2+} + Mg^{2+}]}}$$

- Q = due to exc. K
- Buffering capacity - how K levels in soln (intensity) varies with labile form of element (quantity)
- $BC = \frac{\Delta Q}{\Delta I}$
    = wider the ratio - more buffered — Refer NB for neo diagram

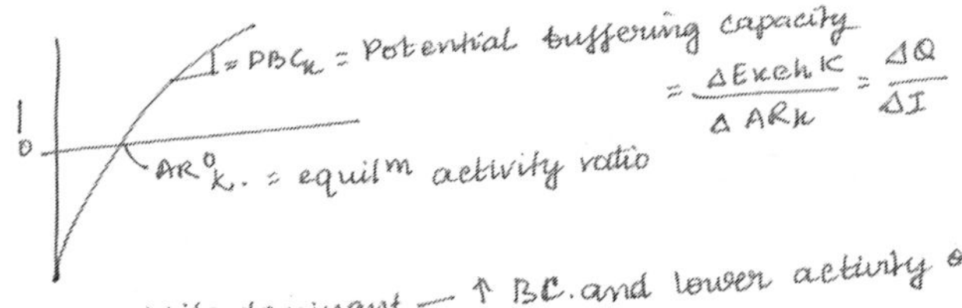

- Soils - smectite dominant — ↑ BC and lower activity of K^+.
    - reverse kaolinite ⟶ for immediate avail.
    - ↳ supply K over a longer period
- with clay ↑, BC ↑, AR_K ↓.

Potassium fixation

- can't be extracted by a neutral salt solution.
- nature of clay important
- absent in kaolinitic, chlorite and unweathered micas

- slight in montmorillonite, substantial in illite
- high in vermiculite

- vermiculite > illite > mont > kaolinite.
- adsorbed or binding sites
- selectivity
- for 2:1 clay minerals — 3 adsorption sites (pie)
  - p-position (planar surfaces)
    - K in OM and clays of kaolinite
    - K bond weak so K easily replaced
  - e-position (edges)
  - i-position (interlayer)
    - maxm specificity
    - largely account for K^+ fixation
    - smectites
    - dehydration - lattice sheets comes closer and adsorbed cation lose their H_2O mol.

- Lattice Hole Theory (Page and Bauer, 1940)
  (laq rod)
  - exposed surface and surfaces between sheets — consist of O ions — arranged hexagonally.
- Opening of hexagon — 2.8 Å (= diameter of O_2)
- K - 2.66 Å
- NH_4^+ - 2.86 Å
- Rb^+ - 2.96 Å

  } Small hydration energies → easy dehydration and retention strong
- Ba^{2+} - 2.70 Å - ↑ hydration energy → can't dehy. and fixed.

- In vermiculite or illite — Isom. subs. creates -ve charge st - explains strength of bond between K^+ and lattice sheet

- Hence, in illite and vermiculite – K fixation can occur even under wet cond.

Factors affecting Potassium fixation

- charge density (-ve charge per unit silicate layer) → ↑ → ↑ fix.
- extent of interlayer wedge zone depleted of K → if confine to edge small fix.
- moisture content → Vermiculite & illite → ↑ more fix → wet condn; Mont → ↑ more fix → dry
- soln K concn
- nature and concn of competiting ions → H^+ and NH_4^+ compete
- Wet and drying → ↑ K.

If zone penetrates deeply → more fix.

Vermi > illite > smectite

Potassium release

- Low hydration energy → favours entrapment
- K^+ concn → low in solution → release of K.
- 2:1 type: - can both fix and release
- capacity of diff cation-saturated resins to replace exch. K^+
  - ↳ H^+ resin > Ca^{2+}-resin > Na^+ > NH_4^+.
  - ↳ more effective in desorbing K from smectite black soils than from alluvial
- exchange of K - diffusion controlled
- kinetics of release of K by Na tetraphenyl boron → Na TPB
  - alluvial soils – illite containing as dominant – release more K than smectite
- capacity of soil to supply K from exch and non-exc. is not easily determined due to reversible transformation
- so, Haylocks (1956) — Step K and Constant Rate K as measure of plant utilizable non-exch K^+.

lag sab

- Step K = release of K^+ with repeated extractions with 1N HNO_3
- Constant rate K → rate achieved when release of K with every extraction = previous one.
  - guide to long term K supply (due to its consideration of soil type and mineralogy)

Usefulness of non-exch. K

- mostly in illite dominant alluvial soils and vermi conta: alluvial and black cotton.
- extractants – 1 N HNO_3
  - NaTPB Na Tetraphenyl B
  - H resins
  - 6 N H_2SO_4.
  - exhaustive cropping.
- Illite/Mica > Vermiculite – major source of non. exch.
- Perennial grasses – rye grass (Lolium perenne)
  - ↳ utilize non-exch.
- Subba Rao — 21 surface soils – basis of non-exch.
- Losses of K
- Luxury consumption
  - ↳ K↑ → Ca↓ uptake
- Leaching and Erosion loss
  - ↳ in coarse textured, organic soils, soils with kaolinite.
- Split appln of K under high leaching
- erosion loss exceeds that of other major elements
  - ↳ 10–55 kg/ha/yr.

Crop Responses to added K

↳ large in laterites, red, red and yellow, mixed red + black.

- K - quality nutrient
- Linked with nutrient interactions than absolute levels of K.
  - K → ↑ best quality tubers in potato
    - protein in cereals and pulses
    - oil content in oilseeds
    - total sugars, sucrose and vit - fruits.
    - sucrose content and sucrose % in sugarcane

- K - improves H_2O use efficiency
  - yield maintain under moisture stress.
  - more tolerant to salinity and alkalinity
  - Potato - withstand frost
  - ↓ fungal attack
  - thicker cuticles and stronger epidermal cells.
  - K - ↓ leaf hopper, brown plant hopper, green leafhopper.

K. INTERACTIONS WITH OTHER NUTRIENTS

- complementary ion effect
  (other cations held on the CE positions of clay)
- K, Ca, Mg - form non-specific function of maintaining ionic balance in plant
- Viets effect - FG. Viets
  ↓
  ↑ Ca concn in outer solution → either ↑ uptake of K, So, tissue K ↑ or ↓ loss of K.

- ↑K → ↓ Mg availability
- (-ve) interaction K × Mg - grapes, canava etc
- ↑K → ↓ Ca or Mg
- K along with NH_4^+ → ↓ Mg of forage grasses
  - ↳ grass tetany (hypomagnesaemia) in cattle
- Na substitute partially K^+.
- Leaching of K^+ in acid, sandy → liming ↑ 6.2-6.5 pH.
- But, appln of high $CaCO_3$ to soil low in K^+ → K deficiency
  - ↳ more in 2:1 clay.

Interconversion
$K = K_2O \times 0.83$
$K_2O = K \times 1.2$ — 0. gem / l. ine

Management of K

- India - no K - rich soluble minerals
  ↳ all imported.
- Muriate of Potash (MOP) - 99% - bec
  SOP (Sulphate) - 1% } fert. use
- MOP - 60% K_2O (50% K) - cheaper, raw material for SOP.
- SOP - 50% K_2O (41.5% K)
- Sensitive crops to Cl^- are tobacco, potato, grapes, fruit trees, cotton, sugarcane, strawberries, cucumber, onion. (apply SOP)
- Oilpalm and coconut - Cl^- loving
- KNO_3 → 44% K_2O (37% K) and 13% N.
  ↳ fruit trees and horticultural.
- Schoenite (double salt of K, Mg) - source of K as MOP for groundnut, banana, [rice, wheat, maize]
- wood ash, manure, crop residues, distillery, coir waste

Methods of appln

- broadcast / spread and mixed
- only - low levels of avail K → band placement or ↑ K fixation.
- some crops - split application
  - monsoon - highly reduced soil
  - rice grown in coarse tex, acid, ↑ rainfall
  - low tillering, late maturing var.
  - where natural supply of K from soil + irrigation ↓ in later stages of growth.

- split appln — sugarcane
  - banana
  - grape vines
  - pineapple
  - papaya
  - tea

FYM / Compost / Vermicom / Biogas | NPK.

Edi

GHG % of gases

- Poultry — 1.16 %
- Biogas — 0.08 %
- Pulse residues – 1.6%
- Rice straw – 1.4 %
- Vermicompost – 0.8 %

Potassium — Tisdale and Nelson

- K – seventh most abundant earth crust (~2.5%)
- absorbed by plants - larger amounts
- Tropical soils → total K low.
- Pools
  - mineral 5000 - 25,000 ppm
  - non exch 50 – 750 ppm
  - exch 40 – 600 ppm.
  - solution 1 – 10 ppm.

- Mineral K = 95-98%.
- available (solution + exchangeable) = 1—3%.
- soil content of total soil K = 0.05 - 3%
- K concn in plants = 1 - 5%.

Functions

- not a component of bio chemical compounds
- so, K functions — related to soln ionic strength in plant cells.
- crop quality – due to involvement of synthesis and transport of photosynthates to plant reproductive and storage organs and conversion into carbohy, proteins, oils and others.
- K deficiency – related to photosynthesis, synthesis and translocation of enzymes.

– affect photosynthesis through

↳ ATP synthesis

↳ prodn and activity of specific photosynthetic enzymes (RuBP carboxylase)

↳ CO_2 absorption through leaf stomates

↳ maintainance of electroneutrality during photophosphorylation in chloroplasts

– K nutrition for optimum photosynth.

↳ measured by CO_2 absorption

↳ varies with crop.

→ 2% leaf K → corn.

– K – Influence stomatal function

↳ ↑ CO_2 absorption

↳ ↑ RuBP carboxy. enzyme activity – combine ribulose biphosphate + CO_2 → 3 – phosphoglycerate – 1st product of CO_2 fixation in leaves.

↳ decrease dark respiration

↳ ↑ of dark resp. reduces plant growth and crop quality.

Secondary Nutrients

Ca, Mg, S → 13th.
↓ 8th
5th abundant

- Ca, Mg - highly electrovalent (small size)
  - so found as abundant cations occupying the exchange sites.
- Activity of Ca - coordination - provides stable but reversible linkage - cell wall and plasma membrane.
- In middle lamellae of cell wall - Ca pectate
- non-toxic, even in high conc - Ca.
  ↳ so, detoxify other mineral elements in high conc.

metalloenzyme, amylase - Ca.
- Ca - mechanical strength to tissue, ↑ cell division and plant growth, protein synthesis, carbohydrate movement and balance cell acidity

	Ca	Mg	S
Atomic mass	(rod) 40.08	(near) 24.31	(man) 32.06
In earth crust (%)	3.20	2.50	0.10
Hydrated ionic (nm)	0.412	0.428	
Hydration energy ($Jmol^{-1}$)	1.5 $kJmol^{-1}$ 1577	1.9 kJ 1908	
Plant conc (%)	0.2 - 1.0	0.1 - 0.4	0.1 - 0.4

Mg - component of chlorophyll (partially covalent)
- activator of enzymes.
- mobility of with in cell → interact with nucleophilic ligands by ionic bonding.
- Mg forms ternary complex → bridging cations between enzyme and substrate
  ↓
  composed of 3 parts

- regulate cell pH
- Ca^{2+} may inhibit activation of Mg^{2+} by displacing it from f-g

Sulphur - sulphides in igneous and sedimentary
- organic compds, industrial wastes, sea waters
- deficient in old deeply weathered land surfaces of highly leached - soils away from sea.
- reqd for synthesis of vitamins.
- reqd for " " 3 amino a
- Proteins - most of S in plant found in it.
- N:S = 15:1.
- Sulphur requirements of crops - similar to P.

Deficiency Symptoms

Ca - rarely deficient
↳ If def. → reduction in meristematic tissue.
→ first appears in growing tips and youngest leaves
↓
Then, necrosis leaf margins.
- In apple - discolouration of fruit meat - bitter pit

- Mg → in coarse textured acid soils.
- Interveinal chlorosis.
- lower leaves - yellowish bronze or reddish.
- In strongly acidic (< 4.5) → reduced absorption of Ca and Mg → cattle feeding on these forages
↓
hypomagnesemia
(Grass Tetany)

- S → inhibit protein synthesis
- yellowing - young leaves.
- nodulation poor.

Sources

Mav Ca and Ma → from weathering

S → OM

95% of total S → OM under temperate cond.

	Total CaO	(%)	Total MgO.
Calcite	56 (sob)		
Dolomite	33 mum		12 live
Gypsum	32 man		
Epsom salt			16 (lab)

Oxidan of S → Thiobacillus

S levels in soils - 30 ppm - 50 ppm

- coarse texture → ↓ S levels. → related with SOM

Sphalerite (ZnS)
Chalcopyrite ($CuFeS_2$)
Cobaltite (CoAsS)
Epsomite ($MgSO_4 \cdot 7H_2O$)

Removal of Sec. Nutrients

- Legume and root crops remove more Ca than cereals and grasses.
- Leaching loss ↑.

S removal - ~~5-8~~ 3-4 kg cereals
~~5-8 kg millets~~
8 kg pulses
12 kg oilseeds.

- S requirement: eg. Cruciferae > Leguminosae > Graminae.

Crucifers > Sesame = Sunflower > Legumes > Linseed.

- Mg^{2+} absorbed less on clay and om than Ca^{2+}
  - ↳ and more susceptible to leaching.
- Generally, soil < 25% ... of CEC or less than 1.5 (<1.5) $cmol(p^+)\,kg^{-1}$
  - ↳ Ca deficient
- soil < 4–15% CEC or less than 1.0 cmol/kg
  - ↳ Mg def.
- Pools

Ca — mineral, exchan, solution

Mg — non-exc, exc, water soluble → behaviour in soils similar to K^+ and Ca^{2+}.

S — total S, organic ← most important (5–98% of avail S), non-organic, available.

Critical limit of $CaCl_2$ (0.15%) - extractable S → 10 ppm.

- Organic S —[O]→ $SO_4^{2-} + H^+$ (so lowers pH)
- Under limited S supply and excess carbonaceous
  - ↳ S immobilized.
- S in soil → C:S ratio of 140:1.
- Optimum temp for mineraliz of S → 35–40°C.
  - moisture → 60% of FC.
- S → more than one oxidation state
  - ↳ so, subjected to reduction-oxidation reaction
- Under anaerobic: partially oxidized cmpds like NO_3^- and SO_4^{2-} → utilized by reducing ...
  - ↳ by Desulphovibrio, Desulphotomaculum
  - ↓ nitrites, nitrous oxide, sulphites, sulphides.

H_2S → under impeded drainage.

Nitrogen

- First member of Group V elements
- collectively, N, P, As, Sb, Bi – pnicogens and compounds – pnictides
  Greek word 'pnigomos' – suffocation.
- N, P → non-metals – form acidic oxides.
- at no. 7 and atomic mass 14.0067
- found as chilesalt petre ($NaNO_3$)
- diatomic in nature
- atmosphere contains 50,000 times more N_2 than soils.
- atmospheric air over each square foot of earth surface – 2700 kg of N. ft^2 – 2700 kg N.
- Elemental N – fractional distillation of liquid air.
- LBP (77.4 °K) than O_2 (92.2 °K)
- more volatile.
- pure N_2 gas – thermal decompos^n of NH_4NO_2 (ammonium nitrite)
- pure N_2 obtained from decomp^n of compounds – led to discovery of noble gases.
- A N_2 molecule – triple bond ($N \equiv N$)

$$NH_4NO_2 \longrightarrow N_2 + 2H_2O$$

$$2N_2 + 5O_2 + 2H_2O \longrightarrow 4H^+ + 4NO_3^-$$ → thermodynamically inhibited otherwise N_2 and O_2 would dissolve in oceans – dilute HNO_3.

Fritz Haber, Carl Bosch } First half of 20th century

- Haber-Bosch process – (see EXTRA).

By passing nitrogen-hydrogen mixture – bed of catalysts consisting of Fe + Metal oxides such as Al_2O_3.

- N_2 AS PLANT NUTRIENT AND POLLUTANT

pools of N_2
- organic (urea, proteins, amines, amides)
- inorganic – mineral (NO_3^- and NH_4^+)
- gas in troposphere (NO, NH_3)

- Total N ~~so~~ in soil ← 0.02 to 0.44 %
- But in general. Indian soils - low in OM - 0.02 - 0.13 %
- N ↓ → temperature ↑.
- N ↑ → relative humidity ↑
- N ↓ → depth ↑.
- N ↑ → virgin soil ↑.
- N ↑ → fine textured

Temp
RH
depth
→ cultivation
fine textured.

- Forms of soil N — organic (98%) / inorganic (2%)
- upto 8% of total N of the surface soils and 40% in subsoil — in clay-fixed form.
- Organic N - mineralized — first hydrolyzable N (Organic N)
  ↳ non-hydrolyzable N resistant
- heavy appln of ferts anaerobic condition, extreme pH, salinity and low temp favour NO_2^- accm in soil.

Soil Nitrogen
- Organic
  - Hydrolyzable
    - Proteins Amino á
    - Amino sugars
    - Acid soluble humin
  - Non-hydrolyzable
    - Insoluble humin
    - fixed NH_4^+
- Inorganic

$$R{-}NH_2 \xrightarrow{+2H_2O} OH^- + R{-}OH + NH_4^+ \xrightarrow{O_2} 4H^+ + \text{energy} + NO_2^-$$

$$NO_2^- \xrightarrow{+\frac{1}{2}O_2} NO_3^- + \text{energy}.$$

NO_3^-

Mineralisation

- Mineralization ↑ in presence of easily decomposable OM.
- " ↓ in presence of lignin complex. (I)

- Aminization
  enzymatic digestion of protein by heterotrophic bac. acti, fungi → amino acids or amines.

Protein → Polypeptides → Amino acids or amines + CO_2 + energy → further ammonification. ↓ immobilized

- Ammonification
  - microbial enzymes - amino a to ammonia.

$$R{-}NH_2 + H_2O \xrightarrow[\text{hydrolysis}]{\text{enzymatic}} NH_3 + R{-}OH + \text{energy}$$

$$NH_3 + H_2O \rightarrow NH_4^+ + OH^-$$ — increase pH especially in flooded.

$$2NH_3 + H_2CO_3 \rightarrow (NH_4)_2CO_3 \rightleftharpoons 2NH_4^+ + CO_3^{2-}$$

- nitrification

$$NH_4^+ \xrightarrow{[O]} HONH_2 \text{ (hydroxylamine)} \xrightarrow{-2H} \tfrac{1}{2} HONNOH \text{ hyponitrite } (H_2N_2O_2) \xrightarrow{[O]} NO_2^- + H^+ + \text{energy}$$

$$NO_2^- + \tfrac{1}{2}O_2 \rightarrow NO_3^- + 20 \text{ kcal.}$$

- $NH_4^+ \rightarrow NO_2^-$
  ↳ Nitrosomonas, Micrococcus, Nitrospira, Nitrogela

- $NO_2^- \rightarrow NO_3^-$
  ↳ Nitrobacter, Nitrocystis.

- popln of nitrify - 1×10^5 to 1×10^7 gm^{-1}.

→ causes acidity.

- presence of excess NH_4^+ → inhibit growth of Nitrobacter (II)
  so accumln of NO_2^-.
- Soil aeration most crucial - 20% (III)
- Moisture content - ½ - ⅓ of WHC (IV)

– nitrobacteria – obligate autotrophic aerobes

– Eh → +250 mV → nitrification occurs (V)

– pH 6.5 – 10.0 but optimum 7–9 avg – 8.5 (VI)

– Temp 25–40°C. (VII)

→ decreases ↑ 0°c =

↓ 50°c. =

nitrification rates doubles for each 10°C rise

– Q_{10} (temperature coefficient) between 5 – 40°c is 2.

– pesticides – deleterious effect (VIII)

C:N ratio (IX)

– of Indian soil 8.5:1 to 12:1 avg. 9.45 ± 0.63

– ratio ↑ with increase in annual ppt

1.5 – 3.5% organic N – mineralizes annually

$$\frac{\text{kg of N mineralized}}{\text{ha in 15cm deep layer}} = \left(\frac{\text{wt of soil}\ (2\times10^6)}{\text{ha 15cm depth}}\right) \times \left(\frac{\text{wt of SOM}}{100\text{ kg soil}}\right)$$

$$\left(\frac{\text{kg N or}}{100\text{ kg SOM}}\right) \times \left(\frac{\text{kg SOM mineralised}}{100\text{ kg SOM}}\right)$$

– $(NH_4)_2SO_4 \longrightarrow 2NH_4^+ + SO_4^{2-}$

– In anaerobic – Two layered

↳ First layer – oxidized

presence of oxidative compds – NO_3^-, Fe^{3+}, Mn^{4+}

↳ Second layer – reduced

NH_4^+, H_2S, Fe^{2+}, Mn^{2+}, organic ā.

– NO_3^- – terminal acceptor of e^-

→ Submerged

- Dynamics of NH_4^+ in reduced soil:

$Co(NH_2)_2 + H_2O \rightarrow NH_2COONH_4$ am. carbamate

$NH_2COONH_4 + H_2O \rightarrow (NH_4)_2CO_3$

$(NH_4)_2CO_3 \rightarrow 2NH_3 + CO_2 + H_2O$

$NH_3 + H_2O \rightarrow NH_4OH \rightarrow NH_4^+ + OH^-$

For high C & N, medium clay & CEC

$Y = a + bt + ct^2$

For low C & N, high CEC & clay

$Y = a + b\ln(t+1) + c[\ln(t+1)]^2$

For medium C & N and medium clay & CEC

$\ln Y = a + b\ln(t+1) + c[\ln(t+1)]^2$

Y = content of avai. NH_4^+ (in ppm)
t = time (in days) after submergence
a = constant
b, c = regression coefficient.

1 kg N →
rice – 68 kg grain
wheat – 44
maize 49

→ Fert N
- NH_4 sulphate (20.6% N)
- NH_4 chloride (25% N)
- DAP (18% N)
- KNO_3 (16% N)
- CAN (25% N)
- AN (35% N)
- ASN (26% N)
- Urea (46% N)

- NO_3^- containing fert must not – anaerobic soil – lost due to denit.
- Urea – breakdown of urea – 3-7 days – one having ↑ C-substrates will proceed faster
- faster in higher pH

Urea — water soluble, leaching loss also.
urease 37°C, 60°C

$CO(NH_2)_2 \xrightarrow[+2H_2O]{Urease} (NH_4)_2CO_3$ ammonium carbonate
under aerobic
↓ anaerobic: dissociate into NH_4^+ and CO_3^{2-}

↑ pH as it prod. NH_3

$(NH_4)_2CO_3 \xrightarrow[2H_2O]{Hydro} 2NH_4OH + H_2CO_3$

$H_2CO_3 \xrightarrow{Autolysis} H_2O + CO_2$

Opt. pH 7.4

Inhibitors – heavy metals

- Farmyard manure (0.5–1.5% N)
  compost (0.5–2% N).

- Green manure – dhaincha — Part in rice
  - sunhemp (Crotolaria juncea)
  - Glyricidia maculata (Green leaf manure)

- faster minera.
- eco friendly
- multiple nutrient
- soil sustain

– takes 45-60 days old.
incorporate – efficiency of fert.
before flowering – before setting seed

- Residues of legumes including roots more better source of N than cereals.
- BNF — Free living BGA (10-20 kg N/ha)
  Azolla (30-40 kg N/ha)
- Energy to break ≡ bond → host plant from photosynthesis.
- $N_2 \rightarrow NH_3 \rightarrow$ α-ketoglutamic ā → glutamic ā
- 21 spp. of Rhizobia.

$$N_2 + 8H^+ + 8e^- \xrightarrow{16\ Mg\ ATP \rightarrow 16\ Mg\ ADP + 16P_i} 2NH_3 + H_2\uparrow$$

cross into infection thread

½ Oxoglutarate + NH_4^+ + ATP + NADPH + H^+ → Glutamate + NADP + ADP + P_i.

- Infection starts when C:N ratio of soil = wide.
- During initial stages, nodules absorb some N.
  ↳ Starter dose apply 15-20 kg N/ha.
- Excessive N appln → harm glutamine synthetase and nitrogenase
- Occurence of red colour leghaemoglobin in nodules — indicates effective N_2 fixers.
- BGA — Nostoc, Anabaena, Calothrix, Aulosira, Tolypothrix, Scytonema, Cylindrospermum, Mastigocladus, Chlorogea
  ↳ neutral to alkaline pH
  ↳ 14-50 kg N/ha/yr
- Azolla pinnata
- Free living — aerobes (Azotobacter, Azospirillum, Beijerinkia, Dersia, Enterobacter)
  anaerobes (Clostridium, Chlorobium, Aerobacter, Methanobacterium, Rhodospirillum, Chromatium, Chlorobium, Rhodomicrobium.

Signalling (flavonoids secreted by roots) → trigger secretion of nod factors → recognised by host plant → infection thread (through crack or intracellular) → triggers cell division in cortex — new organ nodule → release rhizobia → bacteroids

N_2 fixation depends on
- ecotype of legume
- effectiveness of bac. strain
- inor/mineralisa N content of soil
- fert N app.
- adeq supply of P, K, Ca, Mo
- fav soil envn cond.

Leghaem — plant protein — provide O_2 for respiration — keeping low for nitrogenase

	C_4	C_3
	Warm	Cool season plant

- fix less — 5-10 kg N/ha
- C_4 plants (maize, sorghum, forage) - Azospirillum lipoferum
- C_3 plants (wheat, rice, barley, oats, rye) — A. brasilense.
- Trees — Frankia, actinomycetes — Phyllospheric fixation.
  - root nodules
  - (Alnus, Myrica, Casuarina, Comptonia. } non-legumes.
- Mimosa and acacia — leguminous

(C_4): - fix CO_2 → convert CO_2 + Oxaloacetate — 4 Carbon a

(C_3): - directly fix CO_2 directly - enz- RuBPase - chloroplast ↓ 3 Carbon a 3-phosphoglycerate a so, C_3 ↓

- NUE = 750%

Parameters to measure

AR_N: Apparent N Recovery (%)

$$\frac{TU_N - CU_N}{AF_N} \times 100.$$

AE_N: Agronomic Efficiency (kg/ha)

$$= \frac{GY_F - GY_C}{AF_N}$$

PE_N (kg grain / kg N absorbed) = $\frac{GY_P - GY_C}{TU_N - CU_N}$.

(Production Efficiency

Physiological efficiency = $\frac{\text{change in grain yield}}{\text{unit change in accm of N in above ground part}}$ $\frac{dY}{dN}$

→ Fertilizer N residual effect - 15N labelled fert — 65% by above grnd from single appn of 15N fert during first direct crop and 5.7-7.1% in 5 subseq crops.

- Slow release N fert — Urea Super granule (USG) Sulphur coated, neem cake coated, nimin, neem oil coated, polymer-coated.
- Urease inhibitors (PPD) NBPT — N(n-Butyl) thiophosphoric triamide — Agrotain
  - Phenylphosphoro diamidate
- Nitrification inhibitor
  - neem cake, karanj cake, nimin
  - DCD (dicyandiamide)
  - Nitrapyrin / N serve.

(2, chloro - 6 - (trichloro methyl) pyrimidine

AM – 2 amino – 4 chloro methyl pyrimidine.
ATC – (4 amino, 1,2,4 – triazole)
thiourea, hydroquinone, CaC_2

restrict Nitrosomonas – keep N → NH_4^+ form
Refer Npr.

→ LCC reduce → N reqm of wheat and rice by 25%.

→ Foliar appln — waterlogging
— highly percolating coarse texture

→ NDVI (Normalized difference vegetation Index)

→ Ammonia volatilizn – 5-35%.

– less in flooded soil due to dilution of NH_4^+ ion.
– related to partial pressure differ- betwn aq. NH_3 in soil water system and NH_3 in atmosphere immediately above soil – H_2O surface.

$$[NH_3(aq)] = K_H \cdot p \cdot NH_3$$ (Henry's constant)

↑ in NH_3 (aq) → ↑ in pH → loss of NH_3 in atmosphere.

At pH 9.5 → NH_4^+ and NH_3 = same amt (50% each)

→ For each unit ↑ in pH upto 9.5 → 10 fold increase in NH_3 (aq)

→ at Low pH → volati – less.

– Ammonium containing fert → on neutral or acid soil
↓
not much vol.

– But urea → acid soil → more vol.
↓
due to consumption of H^+ during hydrolysis of urea → ↑ pH

– Presence of $CaSO_4$ ↑ → vol. ↑.

- So to reduce ↓, light irrigation after urea app.
- band placement
- more CEC
- coated fert.
- Liming ↑ NH_3 vol.

NDVI.
simple graphical indicator used to analyse remote sensing measurement — assess whether target live green vegetation or not.

- $NO_3^- \rightarrow NO_2^- \rightarrow NO \rightarrow N_2O\uparrow \rightarrow N_2\uparrow$
- ↳ Thiobacillus denitrificans
  T. thioparus
  Micrococcus
  Pseudomonas
  Bacillus
  Achromobacter
- loss from denitrification – 10-40%.
- Chemodenitrification
  ↳ $NO_2^- \rightarrow$ acidic soil
  ↳ NO_2^- + ammonium salts or amino compds.
- C : N ratio of m/o – 8 : 1.
- Diameter of $NH_4^+ \rightarrow 2.96 A^0$
  opening → 2.8.
  $K^+ \rightarrow$ ~~2.66~~ 2.68 A^0.
- Amm. fixation more in subsoil.
- shallow rooted crops → NO_3^- accm.
- 10 mg NO_3–N/L → limit.
- N_2O – 300 times pot. than CO_2.

PHOSPHORUS

- building blocks of genes and chromosome.
- biochemical process.
- component of ATP.
- 1 mole of ATP $\xrightarrow[32 kJ.]{}$ 1 ADP
- Uridine triphosphate (UTP), cytidine TP(CTP) and guanosine TP (GTP) — analogous to ATP.

required for synthesis of UTP — sucrose
CTP – phospholipids
GTP – cellulose

- In synthesis of RNA and DNA
- In seed and fruits → P – phytin
  vegetables → inorganic Phosphate in vacuole.
- Total P content in crop – 0.1 to 0.5%
- Deficiency – growth retardation
  lowering of shoot/root ratio
  poor seed/fruit setting.
- dark green pigmentation on older leaves.
- Group VA
- av. atomic mass = 30.97
  at. no = 15
- P atom can accept 3 electrons or give away 5 e^-
  ↓
  oxidation redn state of –3 to +5
  ↓
  most important in soil.
- taken up mostly as primary orthophosphate ($H_2PO_4^-$) and
  by some plants – secondary ,, (HPO_4^{2-})
  ↑ with ↑ soil pH

- ranks 11th in order of abundance
- mostly as sedimentary fractions or unrefined ore (phosphate rocks)
- co-ppt of 3 molecules of TCP and with one molecule of
  CaF_2, $CaCl_2$, $Ca(OH)_2$ → three apatites
  - $Ca_5(PO_4)_3OH$ hydroxyapatite
  - $Ca_5(PO_4)_3Cl$ chlorapatite
  - $Ca_5(PO_4)_3F_2$ fluorapatite

- In some sedim. deposits → partial replacement of PO_4 by CO_3 in apatite → carbonate apatites or francolites.
- China, Morocco, Jordan . . . PR reserves
- India — Jhamarkota (Rajasthan) — 30% P_2O_5 high grade
- P occurs in mineral as orthophosphate.
- P associated with OM moiety but in non-ortho forms.
- total P content in soil - 200 – 2000 kg/ha in 15 cm.
  with an average 1000 kg/ha.

- For India — 120 – 2166 mg/kg (ppm)
- high in soils with parent material - granite, gneiss & b shales with basic intrusion, limestone.
- Total P → poorly co-related with available P.
  ↳ so rarely used as an index of soil fertility.

Inorganic P

share of In. P to total — 54 – 84%

- P bound to Al, Fe and Ca - major forms
- less active are occluded and reductant soluble forms of P.
- Al-P, Fe-P = acid soils = 1-25% (generally 8 – 10%) of total P
- Ca – P = neutral to alkaline = 40 – 50% or more
- slightly mobile P in sodic soils — associated with Na^+.
- Al, P, Fe-P → more in fertilized soils.
- reductant and occluded → ↑ in acid red and laterite soils.
- P soln concn in soil solution — < 0.1 mg/L
  0.5 kg P_2O_5/ha
- mainly diffusion

→ Al-P and Fe-P fractions – major contributors to plant available P under most situations even where Ca-P is much abundant

<u>Organic P</u>

- 20 – 80% of total P.
- share of – 16% to 46%
- almost nil in desert areas.
- 90% in new alluvial highlands (Assam)
- principal P compds
  - inositol phosphate
  - phospholipids
  - nucleic a
  - other unidentified

- slow release
- <u>Influence of pH</u>

$$H_2PO_4^- \underset{H^+}{\overset{OH^-}{\rightleftharpoons}} H_2O + HPO_4^{2-} \underset{H^+}{\overset{OH^-}{\rightleftharpoons}} H_2O + PO_4^{3-}$$

(strong acidic) ... (strong alkaline)

- <u>Pools</u>

Soil soln P — Surface adsorbed P (labile) — Strongly bonded or adsorbed P (labile) — Very strongly inaccessible mineral / ppt P (non labile)

↓

not slow availability ← bonding very strong; ppt as partially soluble; part of mineral; position within the soil matrix.

	pH
$H_3PO_4 = H_2PO_4^- \longrightarrow$	2
$H_2PO_4^- = HPO_4^{2-} \longrightarrow$	7.2
$HPO_4^- = PO_4^{3-} \longrightarrow$	12.

- Ca-P - dominant in young soil - initial weathering - subsoil.
- as weathering progress → Al-P & Fe-P.

Fertilizer Phosphorus

- being H_2O soluble - forms readily new compds with Ca, Al, Fe, Mn.
- these sparingly soluble cmpd - initial reaction products.
- takes place - in near proximity of the fert.
- value of phos. fert - depends on release of P from initial reaction products rather than fert. per se.
- Reaction product of MCP → brushite } often assoc. with monetite ($CaHPO_4$).
  $Ca(H_2PO_4)_2 \cdot 2H_2O \longrightarrow CaHPO_4 \cdot 2H_2O$.
- another product is ~~ort~~ octacalcium phosphate.
- MCP, Mono ammonium P, mono K phosphate + some black, brown and calcareous → brushite, monetite and taranakite
- In some calcareous soil - cont. Mg — struvite ($MgNH_4PO_4 \cdot 6H_2O$)
  newberyte ($MgHPO_4 \cdot 3H_2O$)
- efficiency of a fertilizer — degree and duration - reacn products can serve as sources.

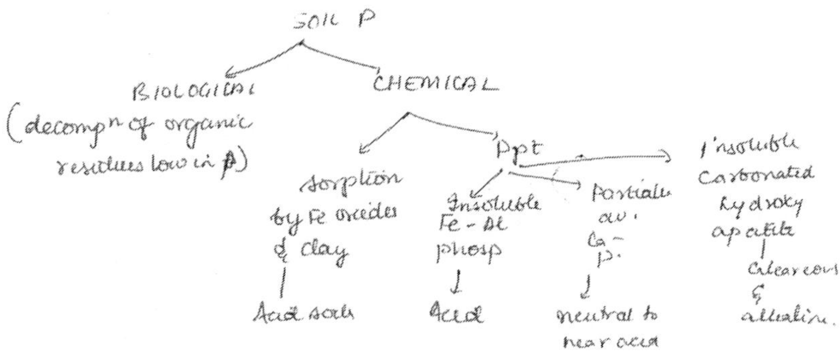

- Effect of Moisture Regime

- flooding → ↑ ~~Al-P~~ reduction of Ferric P to ferrous P

↳↑ availabl. P.

- Organic acids → submerged - solubilize.

- wheat - rice → ↑ avail · P.

→ rice - wheat → ↓ avail P.

→ Al- P ↓ sharply after kharif ~~soil~~ rice

↳ high in high P soil

→ Fe - P ↓ under rice ↪ but ↑ in low P soil

→ Ca - P ↓ decrease due to cropping → ↑ in rice - wheat

- Phosphate fixation

1850 - Thomas Way — soln of $NaHPO_4$ in H_2O and guano in dil. H_2SO_4 → poured over calcareous soil.

- form insoluble $CaHPO_4$.

- adsorption or precipitation

- P ~~ad~~ fixation due to combinatn of — adsorption, chemisorption, ppt

- high pH → TCP → slowly converted to insoluble apatites.

→ low pH — Fe and Al react.

Neutral to alkaline

$$Ca(H_2PO_4)_2 + 2CaCO_3 \longrightarrow Ca_3(PO_4)_2 + 2CO_2 + 2H_2O$$

MCP (soluble) — TCP (insoluble)

Acid

$$Al^{3+} + H_2PO_4^- + 2H_2O \longrightarrow 2H^+ + Al(OH)_2H_2PO_4.$$

Al - hydroxy phosphate (insoluble)

- In neutral to alkaline MCP → TCP → Increase Ca/P ratio
↑. basicity

	Basicity (Ca/P)
MCP $Ca(H_2PO_4)_2$	0.5
↓	
DCP $CaHPO_4 \cdot 2H_2O$ (brushite)	1.0
↓	
octacalcium phosphate $Ca_8H_2(PO_4)_6 \cdot H_2O$	1.33
↓	
TCP $Ca_3(PO_4)_2$	1.5
↓	
Hydroxy apatite $3[Ca_3(PO_4)_2]Ca(OH)_2$ $Ca_5(PO_4)_3OH$	1.67

- where $pH < 4$ → variscite ($AlPO_4 \cdot 2H_2O$)
strengite ($FePO_4 \cdot 2H_2O$)

- Soil temperature → P available ↑ in warm.
- winter crops respond to phosphate fert at high P levels.
- Root grow faster in warm.
- low solubility of P in soil → ↓ movement by diffusion – root zone placement of fert.

- Three types of reactions in P fixation
  - ↳ adsorption
  - ↳ Isomorphous replacement – OH with PO_4^{3-}
  - ↳ double decomposition.

- At low concn of P → ads. isotherm fits Freundlich / Langmuir.
- Reactions of Al-OH and Fe-OH with Phosphate – fixation.

Factors P fixation

- Hydrous oxides of Fe and Al

amorphous Fe and Al oxides → ↑ P fixing capacities than crystalline ones.

- Clays

↑ P fixation — ↑ clay

→ ↑ P fixation → ↑ 1:1 kaolinite

→ ↑ P fixation — ↑ laterite → presence of kaolinite. higher amts of hydrous oxides of Fe and Al.

- Soluble silica

P-sorption ↑ → ↑ soil weathering (decreased Si solubility)

- Amorphous colloids

Amorphous aluminosilicates like allophane → large -ve charge → partly or entirely balanced by complex Al^{3+} cations → P gets adsorbed by reacting with such Al ions.

- $CaCO_3$

Impure $CaCO_3$ and high specific surface (clay size $CaCO_3$) → more sorption of P.

- suspension effect of $CaCO_3$ on extractability of 0.5 M $NaHCO_3$ → de ↓ dissoln of Ca-P; → reppt of dissolved P.

- Cations

More P → sorbed → ↑ valency of exchangeable cations.

Acid soils → retain more P. than alkaline.

neutral soil → " " than saline

Anion

↳ ↓ P sorption capacity in coarse textured. — more effective in calcareous

↳ Among anions — F^- → more effective than sulphate ions.

Supporting electrolyte

With ↑ concⁿ of supporting medium — P retention ↑.
and ↓ with monovalent cation in electrolyte

pH

In strong acid = Al, Fe and hydrous oxides of Fe & Al fixed

moderate acid = hydrous oxides of Fe and Al and silicate clay

slightly acid = " " " " ", " " .

as insoluble Ca-P.

alkaline soil — P initially reacts with Ca — DCP.
↓
Octacalcium P
↙ later
more insoluble
slowly available ← TCP and hydroxyapatite.

Therefore fixation P → not irreversible loss of available P.

Organic Matter

↳ decomp → organic acids → solubilize

↳ → formation of phosphohumic complex (easily assim. by plants)
→ replacement of PO_4^{3-} by humate ion
→ coating on sesquioxide particles.

Temp

↑ → chances P - sorption in soil

Overliming

↑ fixation of P → formation of insoluble Ca-P.

— OM addition

In calcareous — $CaCO_3$ immobilize phosphate

Organic manure — offsets the effect of $CaCO_3$
by keeping reaction products in
metastable or poorly crystalline

- Add^n of green manure ↓ P-sorption
- This effect more pronounced at a high moisture level, strongly acidic and alkaline soil than normal

P- fixing capacity of soils

- black, red, lateritic ; coastal alluvial > alluvial, grey brown, desert.
- $\frac{1}{2}$ of conversion of fert-P → Al-P > Fe-P
- red soil > medium black > heavy black > grey brown > alluvial

P- Buffering capacity

- dynamic relation between labile solid phase (Q) and solution phase → (I)
- measured from slope of isotherm or quantity-I isotherm.
  - ↳ slope at a standard equil^m concn 0.2 μg/mL
  - ↳ . . . . 0.3 μg/mL
  - ↳ max^m slope when conc^n in soln → 0
  - ↳ $\frac{\Delta Q}{\Delta I}$ = differential buffering capacity

- PBC → red soil > black and alluvial
- → So, high PBC → low P conc^n in soln.

- Schofield (1955) – proposing mcp (potential) – best measure of avail P.
  - → quantity
  - ↓ intensity of supply (measured by phosphate potential)

- If Q, I = same units $C = \frac{Q}{I}$ = dimensionless

  Q, I = wt of phosphate per unit volume of soil & soln resp.

  ↓ C = depend on BD of soil.

CQ = constant, where Q/I is linear

$C = \frac{\partial RI^n}{\partial I}$ when conc^n ranges and capacity non-linearly related with intensity

R and n = constants

ln = natural logarithm.

~~the base 10.~~

log = inverse of exponential function 10^x

ln = inverse " " e^x.

$Q = (K_1 c)(K_2 + c)$

c = concentration

K_1, K_2 = constants

- for a given value of intensity, quantity → high in fine textured
- Supply parameter → a dimensionless parameter used to predict the availability of applied P to crops through combined use of quantity, intensity and phosphate buffering capacity.
- $SP = \frac{\sqrt{Qc}}{4\sqrt{K_1 K_2}}$

P. Movement in Soil

- diffusion
- Marschner (1995) - diff. coefficients of $H_2PO_4^-$ → $0.9 \times 10^{-9} m^2/s$ (in water)

10^{-12} to $10^{-15} m^2/s$ (soil)

Avg $10^{-13} m^2/s$.

→ 0.13 mm per day.

slow movement

Available P status

- P fertility problem - 3 fold
  - → low total P content
  - → sparingly soluble - insoluble P compds
  - → fixation of P.
- first compiled by Ramamoorthy and Bajaj (1969) in India

Soil testing for P

0.5 M $NaHCO_3$ pH 8.5 (Olsen et al 1954)

0.03 N NH_4F + 0.025 N HCl (Bray and Kurtz 1945)

Olsen P

< 10 kg/ha = low

10 - 25 kg/ha = medium

> 25 kg/ha = high.

Methods	Suitability
Olsen (0.5 M $NaHCO_3$, pH 8.5)	Neutral, alkaline, calcareous
Bray and Kurtz P-1 (0.03 N NH_4F + 0.025 N HCl)	acidic and near neutral
Bray and Kurtz P-2 (0.03 N NH_4F + 0.1 N HCl)	Tea, coffee, hilly rice.
Nelson (0.05 N HCl + 0.025 N H_2SO_4)	Groundnut
Phosphorus desorption isotherm	Rice.
Electro ultrafiltration (EUF)	Tea.

- Residual effects of P is more than N → beneficial for successive crops.
- ↑ high residues of P → intensive cropping
  - ↳ depends on frequency, rate duration of P fert.
    - solubility of P fert
    - soil prop
    - Types of crops.
  - wheat most responsive

Secondary Nuts contd.

Fe(III) ⟶ Fe(II) } + S sulphide = less soluble sulphides. FeS
Mn(IV) — Mn(II) } MnS FeS and MnS.

In these reductn. oxdn process — SO_4^{2-} last ion to undergo reduction.

It means → to reduce SO_4^{2-} — intense redn necessary
↳ heavy texture - rice - rice - rich in OM — sulphide formation.

Organic S ⟶ SO_4^{2-} ⟶ sulphides, thiosulp, polysulp.

$2S^{2-} + 2H_2O + 3O_2 \longrightarrow 2H_2SO_4 \longrightarrow 4H^+ + 2SO_4^{2-}$ (↓ pH)

- Elemental S → amendment in calcareous soil.

Acid from oxidation of S^{2-} ⟶ dissolving $CaCO_3$

$CaCO_3 + H_2SO_4 \longrightarrow CaSO_4 + CO_2 + H_2O$.

- But not in acid soil.

- Coastal areas - periodic flooding with sea H_2O — extremes of acidity
↓
soil aeration ↓
↓
Sulphur → Sulphides (S^{2-}).

$SO_4^{2-} + 8H^+ + 8e = S^{2-} + 4H_2O$ (increase pH).

- salt tolerant rice - Pokali

- When sea H_2O drained → coastal area — cultivation — oxidization of S^{2-} to SO_4^{2-} and H^+ released → pH ↓.

↳ generally fine textured
- acid sulphate soils / Kat clays
- Kari - Kuttanad region of Kerala
- Sulfaquepts and sulphaquents

- S - adsorption → soils where hydrous oxides of Fe & Al ?.
(ultisol, oxisol, Alfisol)
↳ beneficial (protect from leaching)

- Importance

Ca, Mg — acidic or alkaline

Alkali - 2 Mha India acidic - 25 Mha

Ca → gypsum

replaced Na forms Na SO4 → leached.

$CaSO_4 + NaCO_3 \rightarrow CaCO_3 + Na_2SO_4 \rightarrow$ leached

So, thorough leaching.

- In acid - Ca saturation - 20% - 40%

- acid + oils → non-volatile S glucosides

S in seed - (brassica) - 1.19%.

- Critical limit of S in plants - 0.2 - 0.25%.

- In India - 40% of cultivated area - S deficiency

- oilseeds crops more S reqd.

- N:S ratio : legumes 15, 16:1

cereals 11, 12:1

fert : N:S → 10:1

Soil Classification

- lower category (eg. soil series) — higher category (eg. soil orders)
  - ↳ large no. of differentiating characters / lessens.
- central concept or an idealized individual — (within each class) (typifies the class)
- Evolution

Early system — Economic, Physical, Chemical, Geological, Physiographic.

Soil Classification
- grouping of objects in some orderly | logical
- differentiating characters

Dokuchaiev's Genetic System

- Later part of 19th century
- working in Central Russian Upland — uniform loess parent material extended for 100s of kms with increasing temp. gradient from north to south and and increasing rainfall and moisture gradient from east to west (N → S → temp) (E → W — Rainfall)
- again differences in climate — vegetation — parent material.
- Dokuchaiev — founder of modern Pedology
  - ↳ concept of soil as an independent natural body
- ↳ emphasize on soil genesis — Genetic System of soil classif.
- Dok. (1900) — Normal, Transitional, Abnormal.
  - later: Zonal (from Normal), Intrazonal (from Transitional), Azonal (from Abnormal).
  - Azonal: where time has been a limiting factor to produce fully dev. horizons; eg. Alluvial, Regosols.
- Zonality concept:
  - Zonal: fully developed soil profiles and in equm with the envn. condition. eg. - Sierozem, Chestnut, Podzol, Laterites
  - Intrazonal: within the zonal area but characteristics dependent on local condition, eg. Calcimorphic

Marbut's Morpho-genetic System

- Dokuchaiv's approach - weakness — more importance on climate and vegetation.
- Russian concept - Soil Type (accepted this concept)
- Marbut termed it as Great Soil Group.
- Marbut (1927) — first to classify based on intrinsic properties rather than on soil forming factors

Atlas of American Agriculture
(Based on Fe-Al and Lime contents)

highest category ~~Pedo~~

Zonal → Pedalfers (accm of Fe and Al oxides) → high rainfall areas
Zonal → Pedocals (accm of Ca as $CaCO_3$) → high evaporation areas.

Baldwin and Associates Genetic Systems

- Marbut's disadvantages — assumptions on soil genesis. → some soil series (USA) could not find a place

- Morphogenetic System of Marbut (1935)
  - revised by Baldwin et al. (1938)
  - Kellogg and Thorp (1949)
- marked beginning of comprehensive approach.

Salient features:

- Return to zonality concept
- de-emphazise Pedocal-Pedalfer concept
- emphasize on soil as 3-dimensional body.
- New category Soil family - between Great Soil Group and Soil series.

but neither nor higher categ — defined in terms of soil properties.

– Three orders < Zonal, Intra, Azo. } subdivided – 9 suborders (climate & veg.)
↓
great soil group. (more specific conc.)
↓
Soil families
↓
soil series
↓
soil type.

LIMITATION OF GENETIC SYSTEM

- Two highest categories – genetic terms ↑ not on proper
- concept and definition in highest category – unclear
- Great soil Group – concept and defi- based environ concepts (comparative and qualitative)
- properties described under virgin soil.
- nomenclature on highest cat – too much emphasis on colour or vegetation
- " several languages.
- tendencies to attempt definition of units in lower categories in terms of too few properties//.

SOIL TAXONOMY

- 1960 (9 body) – Comprehensive system of soil classification (7th Approximation) Soil Survey Staff. 1960 starting from 1953 (9 sim)
- 1975 (9 tease) – soil taxonomy (Soil Survey Staff, 1975)
- Salient features (7) – morphology (outcome of soil genesis) act as guide
- Based on properties of soil. (measurable)
- considers properties affecting soil genesis.
- common definition of a class – type or orthotype.
- nomenclature – Greek or Latin
- new category – Subgroup – central concept of Great Group.
- orderly scheme

Diagnostic Horizon → one formed through pedogenic processes – distinct prop – measurable → especially Great Group

↳ surface horizon – epipedons. Greek epi- over, upon; pedon – soil.

- upper most soil horizons and include the topsoil darkened by OM//.

9 epipedons (FAMMOHHPG)

folistic, histic, melanic, mollic, anthropic, umbric, ochric, plaggen, grossarenic

(FAMMOUHPG) FHMMAUOPG

In India most common

mollic, ochric, umbric (more)

KONGS$^{Y}A^{3}P^{3}$ $C^{2}DF$

- subsurface – endopedons (Greek endodermis – sub surface deep seated)

19 endopedons – argillic agric sombric etc. | KONGS$^{Y}A^{3}P^{3}$ $C^{2}DF$
natric spodic cambric

Most - India – (8) – argillic oxic
natric salic
cambic calcic
kandic gypsic

Kandic
Argillic (NAKOSC^{2}G)
Natric

KONG^{2}S^{4}A^{3}P^{3}C^{2}FD

Argillic, Agric, albic, P | Kandic, Oxic, Natric, Gypsic, Salic, Spodic, Sombric, Sulphuric

- Folistic epipedon – never saturated for more than 30 days in normal years.
  - consists of organic soil mat (75% or more) by vol. of Sphagnum fibres
  - or – BD of < 0.1 Mg/m³
  - or – 15 cm or more thick
  - or – Ap horizon – organic (C) content of 16% or more if mineral frac – 60% or more
  - OC content – 8% if no mineral.

Organic Carbon

Histic – High OM (thin) – thinner than 30 cm (if drained) or 45 cm (if not dra)
- remains saturated with H_2O for 30 days or more.

Melanic – thick black horizon → accm of OM | – colour value (moist?) and chroma of 2 or less.
- andic soil properties
- 6% or more OC or 4% or more OC in all layers as weighed average

Mollic – thick, dark, soft mineral horizon
- >50% BS | values > 3 (moist), > 5 (dry)
- strong structure | chroma < 3.5 (moist)
- 1% or more OM

Anthropic – like mollic – long continued use of farms (→ involves large addn of in)
+ 1500 mg or more of citric acid soluble P_2O_5/kg of soil. (1%)

Umbric – like mollic → < 50% BS → ↑ C:N ratio and is not naturally dry for 3 months in a year.

Plaggen – thick – long and continued manuring with sod.
> 50 cm → spade marks → man-made surface
+ artefacts

Grossarenic – sandy horizon (loamy fine sand or coarser)
– 100 cm or more thick over argillic horizon

ENDOPEDONS

Ochric – light in colour (values > 3.5 (moist), > 5.5 (dry))
– < 1% OM
– very hard and massive when dry or remains dry for more than 3 months in a year.

Argillic (Bt) (NB)

- silicate clay horizon – illuviation of clay
- atleast 1/10th of all overlying horizons or more than 15 cm thick.

Natric

- Na enriched
- meet all requirements of argillic but 15% or > of Exchang EC complex sat. with Na^+ or more $Mg^{2+} + Na^+$ than Ca^{2+} + exchange acidity at pH 8.2

Agric

clay, silt and humus – due to long cultivation

Spodic

- humus and/or sesquioxide enriched
- 85% or > of spodic materials.
- Podsols.

Sombric

- illuviation of humus and not of Al or Na.
- free draining horizon.

Cambic

↳ colour or structural B horizon
↳ alteration by physical movement or chemical weathering

Kandic

- low activity clays
- CEC < 16 cmol (p+) kg^{-1} at pH 7
- ECEC < 12 cmol.

Oxic

- Fe and Al oxides with dominant 1:1 clay
- dominance of low charge clays.

H_2SO_4 horizon

- organic/mineral horizon
- pH < 3.5
- yellow mottles of jarosite

Salic horizon

- water soluble salts
- over 2%
- EC > 30 ds/m
- EC x thickness (cm) = 900 or more

Albic

- bleached E horizon — podzols & planosols
- colour values > 5 (dry)
  > 4 (moist)

Glossic

(Gr. Glossa - tongue)

- shows albic charac. gradually intruding into argillic, kandic or a natric

Calcic

Ca, Mg CO_3

atleast > 5% CO_3.

Gypsic

Ca, Mg SO_4

atleast > 5% $CaSO_4$

Petrocalcic

A indurated calcic hor. — hardness of 3 or more

Petrogypsic

strongly cemented gypsic - dry fragments - don't slake in H_2O

Placic

Thin

- dark reddish brown to black
  Fe or Mn pan.

DIAGNOSTIC ORGANIC

Fibric Soil Material (formerly Peat)

↳ fibrous - 2/3 of mass

- clear soln — sodium pyrophosphate

Hemic (mucky peat or peaty muck)

— 1/3 - 2/3

Sapric (muck)

— 1/3

Humilluvic

↳ illuvial humus — some acid organic soil

Limnic

↳ Organic/Inorganic - deposited in H_2O by action of aquatic org.

eg. marl, diatomaceous earth.

Diag. characteri of Mineral and Organic

Aquic (latin - aqua - H_2O) — soil H_2O

Cryoturbation (frost churning) - mixing of soil material - action of [illegible] permafrost table

Densic (L. densus. thick) — thick contact between soil and densic materials - no cracks.
contact

Densic materials - unaltered materials
- don't meet any requirements
- high BD.

Gelic mat — evidence of cryoturbation

Others

Abrupt Textural change

- Durinodes - weakly cemented to indurated nodules, cemented by SiO_2

- Duripan — subsurface horizon - 1/2 cemented by SiO_2.

- air peds don't slake in H_2O or HCl but dest. by hot KOH after acid washing

Fragipan – subsoil layer of high BD.
brittle when moist
Very hard when dry
slake in H_2O

Low chroma mottles – 2 or less chroma
- grey condition.

Permafrost – layer, <0°C

Plinthite (Gr. Plinthose, brick) – humus poor
- sesquioxide rich
- hardens irreversibly to ironstone hardpans.

Soft Powdery Lime – .

Tonguing :– albic → argillic, natric (glossic)

NON-SOIL MATERIAL

Lithic Contact :– Boundary between soil and continuous coherent, underlying mat > 3 moh'sc
root can't penetrate

Paralithic (Lithic-like) Contact : boundary – soil and non-coherent of > 3 moh' - root's can penetrate

Petroferric Contact – soil and indurated layer of Fe cemented

SOIL MOISTURE REGIME

Moist :– Moisture tension < 1500 kPa (15 bar)

Dry – moisture tension ≥ 1500 kPa (15 bar)

within SMCS (Soil Moisture Control Section)
↓
Limit → determined by Soil depth to which the soil at WP is moistened when 2.5 cm and 7.5 cm of H_2O are added.

- Limit of SMCS – 20 cm and 60 cm.
  (in loamy)

- SMR – no. of days SMCS remains moist with moisture tensions between 33 kPa (1/3 bar) and 1500 kPa (15 bar)

- Saturated – aquic
- non-leaching – aridic (water moves in SMCS for short period.
- Leaching – Udic (water moves all round the year)
- Ustic and Xeric
  ↓ Ustic – summer monsoon rains
  ↳ Xeric – winter rains
  } a farmer can grow one crop a year.

- The no. of days SMCS remains moist →
  - moist period (PET < P or P > 0.5 PET)
  - humid period (P > PET)
  - period to evaporate more than 80% of stored avail. moisture after P falls short of PET.

- Thumb rule: – any month – avg. ppt > 50 mm → keep SMCS partially moist

- India – ustic 3/4th (72%)
  aridic (16%)
  udic (12%)

Soil Temperature

Pergelic (L. per – throughout to freeze.) – < 0°C
Crijic (G. kryos: coldness) — 0 – 8°C
Frigid (but warmer) — 0 – 8°C
Mesic — 8° to 15°C
Thermic — 15° – 22°C
Hyperthermic — 22 – 28°C
Megathermic — > 28°C

Used at sub-order
(family).

Diff. MST – MWT > 5°C or more.
If less than 5°C
↓
Iso.

Nomenclature

Order
↓
Suborder
↓
Great Group - based on endodepends
↓
Subgroup — central concept of Grt. Group
↓
Family — land use plants
↓
Series — most specific
↓

- Order. 12 orders AVAGAMI HOUSE
  - ~~ex~~ major diagnostic horizons.
- Suborder (63) — genetic homogeneity
  - wetness
  - climate
  - parent mat.
  - vegetation
- Great group (240+) — diagnostic horizon (exp. Entisol)
- Sub group (1000+) — Typic — central concept of great group
- Family — soil prop — plant growth.
- Series — name after geographic name (200+) in India.

→ sol (L. solum - soil)

'o' → Greek

'i' — Latin

Order	Formative element	Derivation	Mnemoniceon	Suborders
Entsiol	ent	Nonsense Syllable	Recent	5
Vertsiol	ert	L. verto (turn)	Invert	6
Inceptisol	ept	L. inceptum (beginning)	Inception	6
Aridisol	id	L. aridus' (dry)	arid	7
Mollisol	oll	L. mollis' (soft)	mollify	7
Spodosol	od	Gk. spodos (wood ash)	podzol, odd	4
Alfisol	alf	Nonsense	Pedalfer	5
Ultisol	ult	L. ultimus' (last)	ultimate	5
Oxisol	ox	French oxide	Oxide	5
Histosol	ist	Gre. histos (tissue)	history	4
Andisol	and	Jap. and	And	8
Gelsiol	el	Gk. gel, ice	Frost churning	3

3 – G
4 – HS
5 – AEOU
6 – IV
7 – AM
8 – A

8 – Andisol
7 – Aridisol, Mollisol
6 – Inceptisol, Vertisol
5 – Oxisol, ultisol, Alfisol, entisol
4 – Histosol, spodosol
3 – Gelisol

ist od

Gelisol

- Permafrost

Histosol

don't have >30% OM .

Spodosol

Spodic horizon .

Andisol

- andic soil properties

Oxisol

Highly weathered soil - oxic horizon

Vertisol

swell-shrink type

Aridisol

ochric or anthropic epidepon

Ultisols

Low base saturation

Mollisol

Dark colour base saturation (>50%)

Alfisol

H >35% BS - ochric epipedon and argillic/natric or kandic horizon

Inceptisol

- have altered or cambic B horizon

Entisol

- no diagnostic horizon.

- India 329 Mha

Latitudes - 8 - 37

Longitudes - 68 - 97

Peninsula

Extra-Peninsula

Indo-Gangetic Plain.

India - thermic

hyperthermic

Ustic

Aridic

Udic

Alluvial 75 Mha

- parent material - recent origin
- either alkaline or acidic
- least develop horizon
- rich in plant nutrients - P and K
  but low N and OM.
- constraint - stratification - restricts leaching and drainage
  - extreme sandy texture.
  - may be saline.

Entisol
Inceptisol
Alfisol
Aridisol

Black cotton

- on basaltic parent
- 76 Mha
- highclay - 30-80%
- calcareous - 7.8-8.7 pH
- smectite rich
- high BD (1.5-1.8 Mg/m³)
- very fertile

Vertisol

Red soil

Red soil — acidic igneous rock — occupy high topography
Black — basic basalt — low.

Fe - hydration - limonite
- neutral to acidic
- $SiO_2/R_2O_3 \rightarrow 2.5-3.0$.
- deficient in N, P, K, OM, lime
- kaolinite

Alfisol
Ultisol.

Laterite and lateritic

1807 - Buchanan - Malabar Hills.

- Vesicular.
- 25 M ha $SiO_2/R_2O_3 > 2$.
- Kaolin clay

Podsols — deficient in P.

Salt aff — 10 Mha

Solonchaks (saline)

Solonetz (sodic)

- atleast 30 cm
- sandy loam or finer
- low charge clays — CEC < 16, ECEC < 12] pH 7
- gradual increase in clay content than kandic.
- < 10% weatherable minerals in the sand fraction

Sulphuric horizon

- mineral/organic
- pH < 3.5 – toxic to plant roots
- yellow mottles of jarosite

Salic horizon

- secondary accumulation of H_2O soluble salts ($NaCl$, Na_2SO_4 etc.)
- 15 cm thick ⇒ 2% soluble salts
- Product of thickness × salt % = ≥ 60
- ~~Ec~~ salt % in EC — in saturated paste — ≥ 30 dS/m
- Thickness (cm) × EC ~~(cm)~~ (dS/m) ≥ 900

Albic horizon

- bleached E horizon of podzols and planosols
- values > 5 (dry)
  > 4 (moist)

Glossic horizon

(Gr. Glossa – tongue)

- shows albic horizon charac — gradually intruding into
  an argillic
  a kandic
  or a natric horizon } kan
- 5 cm or more thick.
- eluvial parts which const. 15-85% (by vol) of glossic ho. and an illuvial part (ie partially altered or degraded kan).

Calcic horizon

Ca and Mg CO_3

- secondary Ca and mg ~~enriched~~ carbonate enriched
- ≥ 15 cm
- ≥ 15% of secondary accm of carbonates
- atleast 5% more carbonates than underlying horizon

Gypsic horizon

- Ca and $MgSO_4$ enrich
- ≯15 cm thick
- atleast 5% more $CaSO_4$ than underlying.

Petrocalcic

- indurrated (made hard) calcic horizon
- hardness of 3 or more (Moh's scale)
- ½ or more of dry fragments break down in acid, but not in water.

Petrogypsic

- a strongly cemented gypsic horizon
- dry fragments do not slake in water.

Placic

- thin (2-10 mm)
- slowly permeable
- dark reddish brown to black
- Fe or Mn pan lies within 50 cm of the surface.

+ Duripan, Fragipan

(G) Diagnostic Organic materials (5)

Na-pyrophosphate - dispersion agent

- Fibric soil material (peat) — unrubbed condition – over 2/3 of mass
  - clear soln when with Na pyroph.
- Hemic (mucky peat / peaty muck) → 1/3 to 2/3 – intermediate stage of decomp
  - when ex. Na pyro. → values lower and higher in chroma 10YR 7/3.
- Sapric (muck) → < 1/3
- Humilluvic material → Illuvial humus that accumulates after prolonged cultivation of some acid organic soil.
- Limnic material → Organic or inorg. materials deposited in the due to action of aquatic organism or derived from underwater and float org.
  - eg. marl, diatomaceous earth, sedimentary peat (coprogeneous earth).

(5) Diagnostic characteristics of both Mineral and Organic

- Aquic conditions (L aqua - water)
  - continuously or periodically saturated with H_2O
  - reduction
- Cryoturbation (Frost churning)
  - mixing of soil matrix within a pedon
    results
    broken or irregular horizons
    accm of OM over permafrost table, silt capping on rock fragments and oriented rock fragments.
- Densic contact (L densus - thick)
  - thick contact between soil and densic mat below.
  - no cracks.
- Densic materials
  - unaltered materials - don't meet any reqd for other diag hor
  - non-cemented, rupture resistance class.
  - BD not allow root penetration except cracks.
  - dense earthy material - mine spoils, volcanic mud flows till.
  - differs from paralithic (cemented)
- Gelic materials
  - mineral/organic
  - show evidence of cryoturbation.
  - platy, blocky or granular structure

Other diagnostic horizons

- Abrupt Textural change
  - boundary of a considerable ↑ in clay content within a short vertical distance between surface and under-subsoil.
- Durinodes
  - weakly cemented to indurated nodules, cemented by SiO_2.

Duripan

- subsurface horizon
- atleast half cemented by SiO_2.
- air dry peds — don't slake H_2O or HCl
  — but by hot KOH after acid washing

Fragipan

- subsoil layer
- high BD
- moist - brittle
- dry — very hard
- doesn't soften on wetting but broken by hand.
- air dry fragments slake in H_2O.

Low Chroma mottles

- $\leq$ 2 chroma } represent gley cond.
- $\geq$ 4 values

Permafrost

- layer - soil temp < 0°C.
- may be hard or loose.

Plinthite (Greek. Plinthose, brick)

- humus poor
- sesquioxide rich
- hardens irreversibly to ironstone hardpans or aggregates with repeated drying and wetting.
- red. enduring portions — mottle with yellowish, greyish, white red.

Soft Powdery lime

- authigenic lime translocated within the soil.
  ↳ generated where it is found
- as coating on ped surfaces.

Tenguing

- albic horizon penetrates into kan.

Diagnostic contacts to non-soil

- Lithic contact
- Paralithic contact
- ~~Paraferri~~ Petroferric contact

Lithic contact

- soil and continuous, coherent underl. material that has hardness of ≥3 on Moh's scale.
- roots can't penetrate

Paralithic contact (Lithic-like)

- soil and continuous, non-coherent — >3 moh's scale
- root can penetrate at irregular and infrequent intervals.

Petroferric contact

- soil and an indurated layer of iron cemented mat.

Soil Moisture and Temperature regimes

Soil moisture regime

- presence or absence of H_2O ~~at~~ different times of a year.
- soil — moist — moisture tension of < 1500 kPa (15-bar)
- soil - dry - " " ≥1500 kPa (15 bar)

within Soil Moisture Control section (SMCS).

- Limits of SMC — determined by soil depth to which soil at wilting point is moistened when 2.5 cm and 7.5 cm of H_2O are added at surface.
- General - limits — 20 cm and 60 cm.
  - upper (20 cm), lower limits (60 cm)

- Soil physiologically dry – when soil MT is at 1500 kPa or more or when salt concn reaches levels – limits moist. avail.
- SMR – partial function of climate, soil and landform.
  - ↳ no. of days SMCS remains moist with MT between 33 kPa (1/3 bar) and 1500 kPa (15 bar)
- (SMCS) – depth limits of soil that regulates the moisture supply
  - depends on texture.
- SMR – important for moisture supply
  - pedogenesis
  - nutrient availability
  - classification of soils
- 3 dominant moisture regimes. –

i) saturated

ii) non-leaching

iii) leaching

Saturated

- taxonomically aquic • gleying
- soil pores completely filled with H_2O, – anaerobic conditions
- not conducive for normal crop growth.

Non-leaching

- tax. aridic
- water moves into SMCS – short period in year
- completely withdrawn by high PET demand

Leaching

- udic
- water moves into the soil almost throughout the year

- In between leaching and non-l.
  ↓
  ustic and xeric

ustic → indicative of summer monsoon rains (India)

xeric → winter rains (Mediterranean)

farmer can grow one crop in a year

Characterization of SMRs

- runs as SMCS starts moistening when P exceeds 0.5 PET and the supply of moisture to SMCS continues till P falls short of 0.5 PET.
- water need – from storage – continues till 80% of available stored moisture – exhausted by evapotranspiration.
- no. of days SMCS remains moist — (total sum of)
  - a) moist period (PET<P or P>0.5 PET)
  - b) humid period (P>PET)
  - c) period to evaporate more than 80% — after P falls short of PET.
- Thumb rule – any month avg. ppt of >50 mm — 600mm annually keep SMCS/partially moist
- broad SMR – aquic, udic, ustic, xeric, aridic, torric
- India – ustic (72%) – 3/4th, aridic – 16%, udic – 12% } → potential need for addl. irrigation H_2O

12
5
600

Soil Temper

Udic
- moist soils throughout
- To exclude from ustic – not any any part 90 cum. days.
- " " " " xeric – all parts 45 consecutive days of summer solstice

Soils with limited moisture

ustic

Addl. Xeric

Soil Temperature Regimes

Boreal

- Pergelic < 0°C (L. per: throughout, gelare: to freeze)
- Cryic — 0 to 8°C (Gr. kryos – coldness)
- Frigid — 0 to 8°C (like cryic but with warmer)
- Mesic — 8 to 15 (summer than cryic)
- Thermic — 15 to < 22
- Hyper thermic — 22 to < 28
- Megathermic — > 28

Tropical

→ Diff. between ~~MAAS~~ mean summer – mean winter soil temp is 5°C or more.

→ Iso → ≤ 5°C

- Appln: – Used at suborder level

  Distinction betw cryic and frigid – made at subgrp level

  – used at lower (family) level

- < 0°C – no biotic activity
- 0–5°C – no respiration, no root growth, no seed germ — so called inactive.
- 35°C — upper limit of soil temp for root growth
- ~~5–35°C – optimum~~ 5–35°C.
- Temp → family and suborder levels.
- MAST can be computed from MAAT by adding –
  - a) 3.5°C to MAAT for areas between 8° and 16°N latitude
  - b) 2°C . . . . 16° and 26°N
  - c) 1.5°C . . . . 26° and 33°N.
  - d) 1°C . . . . > 33°N.

Soil Taxonomy

Nomenclature

- Basic principles in naming the soils (Heller, 1963) –
  - name must be easily remembered
  - suggest properties
  - suggest place of a taxon in the system
  - short
  - euphonic
  - fit readily in as many language.
- combination of syllables

Structure. Aridisol (L. aridus – dry
solum – soil) – soils of dry places.

Structure

- 6 categories of classification
- Two broad categories – higher and lower
- based on morphology

Higher

- Order – highest (12) AVAGAMI HOUSE – presence/absence major diag. horizons.
- suborder – comparable to great soil grp of genetic sy.
- great group – basic category, based on diag. subsurface

(63)

Lower

- subgroup – central concept of great group
- family – making predictions for land use plans
- series – lowest but most specific.

Subgroup – intergrades between two great groups.
- extragrades transitional to not soil pop.
- emphasise soils are in continuum – with gradual changes in morphology and soil properties.

soil type – dropped in favour of soil phase.

→

Differentiating characters

- Order (12) - AVAGAMI HOUSE
  - presence or absence of major diagnostic horizons
  - based on morphology.
- Sub order - 63
  - emphasize genetic homogeneity, wetness, climatic environment, parent material and vegetational effects
  - mostly temp and moisture regime.
- Great group (240+)
  - based on diagnostic horizons (except in Entisol - no horizon)
  - soil temp and moisture regimes.
- Sub group (1000+)
  - Typic — define central concept of great grp
  - Others — indicate intergraded to great groups, suborders and orders.
  - extragraded - not soil.
- Family - soil properties like texture, minerological class, soil temp, pH.
  - land use planning.
- Series - lowest category
  - ~~Soil individu~~ collection of soil individuals, essentially uniform in differentiating characters and in arrangement of horizons.
  - most useful for land use plans.
  - named after the geographic area where it first recognized. or exide extent.

Appln of Differentiating character

- common ending of orders – sol (L. solum. soil) –
- connecting vowel 'o' for greek
  'i' for Latin and other roots.

- each suborder – two syllables.
  - first suggestive of a property of class
  - second the name of order (formative element)

  - udoll – udic – Mollisol
  - xerert – xeric – Vertisol
  - fluvent – fluviatile – Entisol.

- Great groups – one addl. prefix to suborder
  - Hapl-udoll

- sub group – name of great group modified by one or more adjectives
  - Typic hapludoll

Name of order	Formative element	Derivation of forma. elem	Mnemonicon	Soils equivalent in other systems
Alfisol	alf	nonsense	Pedalfer	Podzolic (grey brown) degraded chemozem
Vertisol	ert	L. verto (turn)	Invert	Grumosol Black cotton soil (Regur)
Aridisol	id	L. aridus (dry)	arid	desert, sierozem, solonchak
Gelisol	el	Gk. gel (ice)	Frost churning	Frozen tundra
Andisol	and	Jap. and	Ando	Volcanic ash soil.
Mollisol	oll	L. mollis (soft)	mollify	chestnut, Chernozem, Brunizem, Rendzinas
Inceptisol	ept	L. inceptum (beginning)	Inception	Forest Humic gley soil
Histosol	ist	Gr. histos (tissue)	histology	Bog soils
Oxisol	ox	French oxide	oxide	Laterite, Latosols
Ultisol	ult	L. ultimus (last)	Ultimate	Red yellow Podzolic Half bog, Planosols.
Spodosol	od	Gr. spodos (wood ash)	Podzol	Podzols (Brown and Ground H_2O)
Entisol	ent	nonsense	recent	azonal

non-sense syllable – entisol and alfisol.

ENTISOLS (recent)

Concept

- recently developed mineral soil
- no diag. horizon other than ochric or anthropic epipedon
- slight degree of soil formation/profile development
  ↓
  due to either limited time for develop. or extreme texture, exceedingly unfavou condition or topo
- unaltered original crystalline, metamorphic or sedim. features of parent material.
- variable parent mat — recent alluvium (sand dunes) to variety of rock.
- topography varies — floodplains/on steep slopes.
- under varying climatic conditions.

varying parent mat. topography climate

Classifn

AFPAO

SO → 5

- aquents – aquic con
- fluvents – fluvial nature (recent flood plains)
- psamments – extremely sandy (sand dunes of Rajas) (AFPAO)
- arrents – fragments of dia hori within one metre
- orthents – well drained non-fluviatile (rocky humid or subhumid moun. of Himachal Prad)

Land use

- some are rocky steep slopes – trees
- too stony, infertile or poorly drained
- large areas – alluvial bottom lands – veg. and grain cult – pasture.
- interdunal areas – one crop in a year.

Distribution

- widely distributed – occur anywhere where time, extreme texture, erosion, extreme slope – limiting factors
- mainly on steep slopes, flood plains along streams and near oceans
- in arid, sand dunes area.

–

INCEPTISOLS (L. inceptum – beginning)
(ept)

Concept

- early stage in soil formation
- Entisol (least developed)
- may have some accm of clay in subsurface – but not suff. for argillic horizon
  ↓ which is for alfisol / ultisol.
- may have dark surf. colour
  ↓ for mollic epipedon
  ↓ mollisols.
- not usually dry
- have one or more of diag. horizons (cambic, umbric or mollic) (cum) with low base saturation
- developed recently owing to the alteration of parent material to develop soil structure – but without much leaching & accm of mat in subsoil.
- throughout the world.
- In India, all over except hot and arid regions.

classifn

- 6 suborders – A^2U^2CX

- aquepts – aquic
- anthrepts – plaggen/anthropic epipedon
- cryepts – cryic temp
- ustepts – ustic mois
- xerepts – xeric moi
- udepts – udic soil mo.

Land Use

- agricul. productive
- excellent natural grazing grounds.
- pasture and veg + grains.
- in general, product.
- however, some are limited – due to imperfect drainage/sodicity.

VERTISOLS (ert)

(L. verto, term meaning invert)

Concept

- derived from morphological manifestations
- uniform thick (atleast 50 cm)
- black and other dark colour.
- cracking clay mineral - > 30% of clay
- swells - wetting - shrink - drying.

develop of wide deep cracks ass. with gilgai microrelief or intersecting slickenslides.

- India, NE Africa, Australia, Southern USA
  - MP, AP, Maharashtra, Gujarat ..

Classfn

- 6 suborders ~~(U²CXAT)~~ TAU²CX

- Aquerts
- cryerts
- xererts - open > 60 cons. days.
- Torrerts - cracks remain closed < 60 cons. days (when soil temp > 8°C)
- usterts - open for > 90 cumulative days.
- uderts ..

~~Land~~ use constraints

- shrink and swell charac - pose tillage problems, for building, drainage and gas pipe lines, installing irrig networks.
- Tilting of trees, fences, sinking of floor - charact.
- ~~noexcellent natural~~ gra.

Constraints

- Land use
- natural grazing (excellent) - with irrigation - 2 crops in a year
- under rainfed - one crop - cotton, sorghum, pigeonpea.
- lower topog - rice.
- productive, provided good management.

MOLLISOLS (L. mollis meaning soft)
(olls)

Concept

- soils of grassland
- under subhumid (semi arid, moist) to humid.
- dark colour, well developed, base rich, well structure surface horizon — rich in OM (mollic epipedon)
- subsurface horizon — rich in illuviated clay (argillic or Bt)
  - calcareous (calcic or Bk)
  - gypsiferous (gypsic or By)
  - but not definitive of Order.
- result from decomp. of organic mat — roots of grassy veg — diverse earthworm.
- mostly in central USA, Russia, Central South America.
- India — Tarai region of UP and Uttarkhand
  - some in Himalayas.

Classification

- 7 suborders. (~~A^2U^2CXR~~) RA^2U^2CX
- albolls — albic bleached horizon over an argillic / natric.
- aquolls — aquic.
- ustolls
- udolls
- cryolls
- xerolls
- Rendolls — > 40% $CaCO_3$ content within or below mollic ep.
  - aridic soil mois.
  - cryic soil temp

Land use

- inherently best agri soil.
- In India — optimum yields-
- in drier regions — use for grazing.
- subhumid — variety of crops — wheat, maize, veg.
- Tarai region (UP and Utt) — due to summer monsoon rain — maize and sorghum

ARIDISOLS (L. aridus - dry)

(ids)

Concept

- mineral soils of dry areas and having high ground water table
- remain dry for most part and salts accm
  ↓
  calcic, gypsic or salic horiz
- South Asia, north and NE Africa, Australia.
- India – Rajasthan, Gujarat, Haryana

Classfn

7 suborders:–

[C³SADG]

- Cryids
- Calcids – calcic / petrocalcic
- cambids : other common type.
- salids :- salic
- argids – argillic / natric starts within 1 m of surf.
- durids :– duripan within 1 m
- gypsids – gypsic / petrogypsic.

Land Use

- don't support crop without irrigation
- If irrigation also – salinity problem – sink holes develop in gypsiferous.
  ↓
  due to dissolution of gypsum
- In non-gypsifer → one crop (usually pearl millet) – ~~ft~~.
- except ~~so~~ halophytes

ALFISOLS (from Pedalfer of Marbut)
(alf)

Concept

- base rich, timbered mineral soils - subhumid and humid.
- light colour surface (ochric epipedon) — over ~~clay~~ argillic subsurface.
- Alfisols - less weathered than ultisols.
- ~~India~~ USA, South America, Northern Europe.
- India - Red soils - AP, Assam, Arunachal, HP, Maharashtra

Classfn

- 5 suborders.

~~A²U CX~~ AC ~~AU²~~CX

XACU²

- Aqualfs
- Ustalfs
- Udalfs
- Cryalfs
- Xeralfs

Land use

- high base saturation
- favourable texture and location } fertile and productive
- semi arid to humid
- for forestry, grazing also.
- fruit, veg and grain
- wheat, maize, sorghum
- hort - mango, litchi, cashew
- Na rich Alfisol - amelioration - appl of gypsum

SPODOSOLS (od)

(Gr. spodos – wood ash)

- mineral soils
- accm of sesquioxides and humus – subsurf.
- cool, humid climate
- coarse-texture siliceous parent mat. favours free leaching.
- illuvial horizon, enrich with free sesq. (Bs) and humus (Bh) underlying a bleached, wood ash colour eluvial E horizon
- NW Europe, N and NE USA, Canada
- India - seldom reported

clasif

- emphasis more on B-horizon than E.
- 4 suborders :–

ACHO

- aquods – aquic
- cryods – cryic
- Humods – high > 6% OC
- Orthods – other common types.

ULTISOLS

(L. ultimum – last)

- comparable with Alfisol → > 35%.
  low base saturation < 35%) reason
- (more weathered
  advanced stage of weathering.
- base poor, timbered, mineral soils.
- humid – high rainfall > forest veg.
- ~~cla~~ argillic subsurface or kandic horizon.

- warm, humid and subtropical regions.
- south east USA, South America, South east Asia.
- Kerala, Tamil Nadu, Orissa. Assam and some north eastern states.

Classfn

~~AU~~ XH

UHUXA

- 5 suborders.
- aquults
- humults — high OC — 12kg/m² or more.
- udults
- ustults
- xerults

Land use

- low fertility and low base status
- low productivity
- forestry — some good agri and plantation crops — limed and fertilized.
- In tropical sr regions - pineapple, sugarcane, coffee

OXISOLS (Fr. oxide - oxide)

- strongly and deeply weathered mineral soil.
- humid tropics
- poor in fertility
- uniform profile - dominated by kaolinite, sesqui deep subsurf.
- plinthite also develop (may)
- most have brick red colour, some are yellow or grey.
- in tropical areas -

  Central Africa, & NE South America, SE Asia

- India - not reported yet.

Classfn

- 5 suborders ATUUP
- Aquox - aquic
- Torrox - aridic moisture
- Ustox - ustic or xeric
- Udox - all udic
- Perox - perudic moisture regime

Land use

- chemically degraded soils
- need careful management for agri. use
- grazing and forestry.
- growing crops - coffee, rubber, cocoa, sugarcane and

  fruit crops - pineapple, coconut.

- Shifting agriculture (especially shifting cycle > 20 yrs)
-

HISTOSOLS

(Gr. histos, meaning tissue)

Concept

- soil formed on organic soil material.
- thumb rule :- soil without permafrost – histosol if half or more of upper 80 cm is organic.
- called histosols, if organic materials rest on rock.
- organic rich soils with thick, peaty horizon (histic epipedon) – develop in lower topographic positions in a permanent water saturated environment
- main process – accumulation of peat
  - when OM produced by native veg is more than OM decomposition
- rate of peat accm in soil – 0.5-1mm per year
  ↓
  rate much slower in swamps than herbaceous veg.
- amount of OM reqd for soil to qualify – depends on clay content
- minm amot of OM is 20% if clay content is nil.
- Northern parts of Europe, northern USA, Canada
- India – Kerala, Tripura, Andaman and Nicobar Islands.

Classification

- Four suborders :- HFSF
- Hemists, Fibrists, Saprists and Folists

Land Use

- esp. Fibrists – located in depressions and flat areas.
  Folists – freely drained
- vegetables
- Hemists – show moderately decomposed OM and are used for vegetative cover
- drain these soils → they oxidise and subside, making the drainage difficult.

ANDISOLS (from Japanese — black soil)

Concept

- first recognised in Japan and were named as Volcanic ash mat.
- central concept - developed on volcanic ash.
- dark colour, & low bulk density soils — don't have an albic horizon
- must have andic properties (loose or friable, colour, mollic or umbric surface horizon overlying a brown cambic B horizon and/or one or both of the following: —

  low BD (< 0.9 Mg/m³)

  or 60% or more vitric volcanic ash within 60 cm
- typical characteristics — high content of allophane —
  ↓
  low B.D and fluffiness, esp. in B-horizon
  ↳ makes them easy to cultivate.
- on all topographic positions and under all mois and temp.
- Japan, New Zealand, Indonesia and Philippines.
- India — Andaman and Nicobar Islands.

classfn

- 8 suborders ((AU²CX TVP) TAU CUX V

- aquands —
- cryands —
- torrands —
- xerands —
- vitrands — durpan or a petrocalcic
- ustand —
- udand —

Land use

- on steep slopes - limited mechanized farming.
- in fav. climatic cond - thickly populated — intensi cult.
- adv. to grow crops (showing little response to app of P)
  ↳ sweet potatoes (Ipomoea batata)

- Reason
  - high P fixing capacity.
- stable and resist water erosion — due to ↑ ~~filtro~~ infilt. and permeability rates
- when dry - susc. to wind erosion

GELISOLS
(from gelic - frost churning)

- most recently introduced.
- permafrost - extreme northern hemisphere.

Concept

- with gelic materials, underlain by permafrost. (mineral or organic ~~m~~ soil mat. show evidence of cryoturbation)
- dig. hori — may / mayn't be present
- due to ↳ freezing and thawing.
- Permafrost influences pedogenesis — ~~by a~~ as barrier to downward movement of soil solⁿ.
- Northern USA, Canada, Russia.
- India — not reported
- may observed in higher Himalayas.

Classfⁿ

↳ 3 suborder (HOT)

- Histels - organic soil mat. or are sat. with H_2O for 30 or more in a year.
- Orthels - other common type
- Turbels - show cryoturbation in form of irregular, broken. horizon boundaries.

Land use

- not cult.
- left for natur. veg.

Advantages and disadvantages (Soil Taxonomy)

- Advantage
- primary basis for identifying - properties that exist in field.
- nomenclature - gives definite connotation of major soil char.
- in built mechanism to permit addⁿ of new soil groups, suborder or even new order without being disturbed.
  eg. Gelisol and Andisols.
- permits classification of soils rather than soil fo. process.
- focus attention on soil rather on related sc.
- permits clasfⁿ of soils of unknown genesis
- permits greater uniformity of clasfⁿ as applied by scientists located far away.

Applications
- most logical soil clasfⁿ
- goal - help soil survey
  - in making predictions - by assesing potential and constraints
  - agro tech transfer.

MAJOR SOILS OF INDIA

- India located - latitudes

~~dr~~ 8° 04' and 34° 06' N.

gdr — mr.db longitude

bg.dat — qot.nose 68° 07' to 97° 25' E

g dr
mr db
bg dt
qt ns

- geographical area - 329 mha
- Physiographically - 3 broad regions
  - Peninsula (triangular Plateau in Deccan and south of Vindhyas)
  - Extra Peninsula (mountain region of Himalaya)
  - Indo-Gangetic Plain

Peninsula

↳ great part occupied by Archean rocks - comprising gneiss, schists and other rocks.

↳ Red soils (Alfisols) ~~d~~ predominant

Extra Peninsula

- shows devlp. of marine sediments of all ages. especially north of Himalayas
- major rock :- tertiary old sedimentary (sandstone, limestone) igneous (granites)
- non-calcic brown soils predominate

Indo-Gangetic Plain

- composed of alluvium of the great river systems.
- alluvial soils
  - Entisols or Alfisols (based on age of alluvia degree of development)
  - Inceptisols

- India - three district seasons: —
  - viz. cool and dry winters — Nov - Feb.
  - hot and dry summer — Mar - June
  - monsoon rainy — mid June - Sept

Rainfall
- south west monsoon (June to Sept)
- north eastern winds (Dec - Feb)

- Western Ghats and eastern himalayas - receive max^m rainfall
  ↳ due to their alignment across summer monsoon winds.
- Indo Gangetic Plain - moderate rainfall
  Rajasthan - little as the Aravallies lies along the path of moisture bearing winds.

- Temp - 42°C-47°C during summers (May-June)
  ↓
  falls with onset of monsoon rain (July-Sept)

- Bioclimate - climate prevailing a few metres above and below the soil surface where bio activity prevails.

- India - thermic and hyper thermic
  - ustic, Aridic, udic
- Grouping of soils
  - Genetic System (genetic factor)
  - Soil Taxonomy (soil properties) - measurable

ALLUVIAL SOILS

- soils developed in alluvium (irrespective of place of occurence and degree of development)
- imp in agri production.
- Punjab, Haryana, UP, Uttarakhand, Bihar, WB, Assam, coastal regions.
- 75 Mha in Indo-Gangetic Plains and Brahmap. valley alone.
- parent material - recent origin.
- derived from deposition - erosion products - river systems
  - coastal alluvium - sea currents

Salient charac

- variable in texture (depend - parent mat and place of deposition)
  ↳ coarser near the source and finer in proximity to sea.
- fluvial in nature (stratified) - reflected in texture
  - irregular dist. of OM with depth.
- either alkaline or acidic (udic)
  (ustic/aridic)

- exhibit different profile developments from least deve. AC to well developed ABC.
- rich in plant nutrients
- fairly suff. for P and K
- deficient – N and OM.

clasfn

- In genetic — Azonal Soil Order
- Taxonomy – Entisol (with AC profile)
  Inceptisol (with A-(B)-C)
  Alfisol (with A-(Bt)-C)
  Andisol (with A-(B)-C)

Land Use

- of major constraint - stratification – restricts leaching and drainage.
- extremely sandy – excessive leaching of H_2O and nutrients
- hydromorphic condition — reduction - poor aeration.
- if managed – rendered useful veg crops and agri crops.
- render saline if evap exceeds rainfall (aridic zone)

BLACK (COTTON) SOILS

- very dark – extremely hard on drying – sticky and plastic on wetting
- difficult to cultivate
- comparable with Grummosols of USA, chernozems of Russia, Prairie soils of USA
- India — central, southern and western
- 74 mha
- characteristic shrink-swell characteristics
- developed on basaltic material under semi-arid to sub-humid
- ~~na~~ tropical dry deciduous and tropical thorny forests with fairly growth of grasses.
- weathering product of parent mat. (basalt and other met. rock containing lime and soda -lime feldspars)
  ↳ are basic and rich in clay (smectite)

- smectite - expansion and contraction - steady churning process in pedon
- churning causes vertical mixing in deep soils - lead deep cracks (>50 cm) and wide (> 1 cm) cracks, gilgai micro-relief and/or closely intersecting slickenslides.

Salient charac

- high clay content - 30% - 80%
- being calcareous - pH 7.8 to 8.7 → upto 9.5
- rich in smectite - high exch capacity (30 - 60 cmol (p+) kg⁻¹ soil)
- high H_2O and nutrient holding cap
  - ↳ 150-250 mm/m - large part not available for pla growth
    - tenaciously held by smectite.
    - reduces permeability and poses drainage problem
- don't exhibit any eluviation and illuviation
  - due to churning
- high BD (1.5 - 1.8 Mg/m³) - due to swell-shrink.
- dark in colour - due to clay-humus complex
  - presence of titaniferous magnetite mat
- highly sticky and plastic

classfn

- Genetic System - Intrazonal, Azonal (Regosols, alluvial)
  (Grumosols, regur)
- Taxonomy - Vertisols (deep, black)
  - Usterts, Torrerts (sub orders)

shallow soils - Inceptisol
- Entisol.

Land use

-

Mineral Nutrition of Plants latest – ununpentium at no 115

- 119 - identified - included in Periodic table
- Nutrient — one - required to complete life cycle - organism - relative deficiency - specific def. symptoms.
- essentials deficient — so low - severely limits growth.
  - produces def symp.
- Insufficient — ass. with growth reductions
  - but no def symp.
- Optim Sufficient — range of nutrient content &
  - ass. with optimum growth and crop yields.
- Toxic - concn too high
  - sig. growth reductions
- Available nutrient
  - fraction
  - variation in amt - responsible for - sig. changes in yield and response (Bray, 1948)
  - depends not only their chemical. physical nature of soil but also ability of plant to forage them - root system.
  - only a small portion of total nutrient
- Bioavailable nut
  - nutr. available to biological organisms.
  - portion of nutrient in soil - readily absorbed and assimilated by plants (avail. nutrient).
- Beneficial elements
  - mineral elements - stimulate plant growth
    - not essential for or which are essential only for certain plant sp. or specif. condition
  - Si, Na, Al, Se, Co, Va
- Functional nutrient
  - Nicholas (1961) - full name of — DJ Nicholas
  - elements - role in plant metabolism whether or not role is specific or indispensable.

Trace elements
- element found in low concn
- < 1 ppm or still less in soil, plant, water e

Tracer element
- radioisotope or stable isotope of an element
- for tracing its path in a system — to study mechanism of its interaction with system — tracer.

Heavy metal — relative density = density of sub / density of H_2O
- sp. gravity > 5. or atomic no > 20
- any metal heavier than ca.

Nutrient content
- concn of nutrient or its amount per unit wt of plant tissue
- exp. as % — kg/100 kg or g/100g or ppm (parts per million) — mg/kg of dry matter or µg/g of dry m.
- ppm = % × 10^4.

Nutrient accumulation
- Storage — nutrient — particular part or portion of plant

Nutrient uptake
- amt of nutrient taken up by growing crops from soil or other sources.
product of plant matter produced × nutrient concn in plant

N. removal
- Nutrient contained in harvested portion of crop.

ESSENTIAL NUTRIENTS — D.I Arnon & PR Stout
- elements needed by plants — without which — not able to survive.
- must satisfy criteria — propounded by Arnon and Stout (1939)
  - deficiency of an esse. — makes it impossible — complete the veg or repro. stage of its life cycle
  - def. is specific to the element — can be prevented or corrected only by supplying that element
  - involved directly in nutrition of plant, quite apart from possible effects in correc. some microb./chemical condition of soil/culture medium

- 17 nutrients essential

- C, H, O
- N, P, K
- Ca, Mg, S
- Fe, Mn, Zn
- Cu, Ni, B, Mo, Cl.

Plants

For humans?
how many essential elements

9 amino ā
2 fatty ā
13 vitamins
15 minerals
(39) (20)

- latest addition 1987

Macronutrients

- major nutrients
- are so called reqd in large quan. more than Iron.
- C, H, O, N, P, K, Ca, Mg, S. < Primary / Secondary.
- 90-95% of plant drymatter wt
- supplied through CO_2 & H_2O.

Primary

- N, P, K
- so called - larger requirements
  - correction of widespread deficiencies
  - appln of commercial fert.

Secondary

- Ca, Mg, S
- moderate requirements
- localized deficiencies.
- corrected - incidental accretions through carriers of primary nut. nut.
  - eg. P-fert - SSP < Ca, S. + P.
  - Amm. sulphate - N + S.

Micronutrients

- need in relatively smaller quant.
- Fe, Mn, Zn, Cu, B, Mo, Cl, Ni (8)
- absence of one atom of Mo — 60×10^6 — H
  - 30×10^6 — C
  - 30×10^6 — O atoms
  - 10×10^5 — N
  - ineffective from plant nutrition point of view

- Micronutrients
  - Cations (Fe, Mn, Zn, Cu, Ni) – 5
  - Anions (B, Mo, Cl) – 3

depending upon form plants absorb.

Functions and deficiencies

Why rice take up as NH_4^+ and others as nitrate? anaerobic

glutamine synthetase in rice root can use ammonia

- Nitrogen – 7, 14.
- NO_3^-. rice – NH_4^+
- N-sufficient plants – 1-5%
- most often deficient in soil.
- creates serious nut. problems

Functions

- major component of a plant cell and cell wall – 5% N
- ess. comp. of amino acids, proteins, nucleic ā, porphyrins, flavins, purins, pyrimidine nucleotides, flavin nucleotides, enzymes, co-enzymes and alkaloids
- chlorophyll.
- part of nucleic ā – RNA, DNA — transfer of genetic code to offsprings
- improve quality of leafy veg. and fodders.
- improves protein quality of foodgrain – by
  ↑ glutamic ā, proline, phenylalanine, cystine, methionine, tyrosin
  ↓ lysine, histidine, arginine, aspartic ā, threonine, glycine, valine, leucine in grain

WACNLP
↳ Cell wall
↳ amino ā
↳ chlorop
↳ nucleic ā
↳ Leafy
↳ Protein

lysine is a bad protein?

Def. sym

- < 1% N content – plants regarded deficient
- Stunted growth – manifestation
- highly mobile – appear on older leaves (light green to pale yellow colouration (through proteolysis)
- reduction in flowering and crop yields
- ↓ protein content

Excessive consumption

- succulence ↑ → more insect and pest attack
- taller plants & heavier heads – lodging

Phosphorus

- P — 15, 31
- second most abundant in human body — 20% of body's minerals
- plants - dihydrogen orthophosphate ($H_2PO_4^-$)
  but neutral to alkaline monohydrogen orth (HPO_4^{2-})
- 0.1 - 0.4% by weight in plant ie 1/5th - 1/10th of N & K content

Func

- P incorporated into nucleic ā (RNA, DNA), nucleop phosphoproteins, phospholipids, sugar phosphates, enzymes and energy rich adenosine triphosphate (ATP), ADP —
  ↳ energy currency of plants
  - ATP stores 12 kcal energy per mole contained in 2 pyrophosphate bonds between 3 P molecules

MEN PGSN
↳ metabolic process
↳ energy
↳ Nutrient m
↳ Photos
↳ Genetic
↳ Sugar
↳ Nucleic ā

- ATP involving metabolic process: —
  - generation of membrane electrical potentials,
  - respiration,
  - biosynthesis of cellulose, hemicellulose, pectins, lignins, proteins, lipids, phospholipids, nucleic ā

- P involved in energy transfer — photosynthesis
  - photosynthesis (RuBP) RuBisCo carboxylase oxygenase
  - transformation of sugar and starch
  - nutrient movement within plant
  - transfer of genetic char. from one generation to other

RuBP
Ribulose 1,5 biphosphate

Def

- < 0.1% — P deficient
- faster mobility - older leaves.
- ass. with acc. of carbohydrates — results prodn of dark green colour leaves.
- severe restriction in growth of plant tops and roots
- thin, erect, spindly with sparse and restricted foliage

- as develop. of lateral buds suppressed - leaves - narrow - acute ∠ with stem axis - foliage bluish green.
- under continuous def - older leaves - bronzed or develop reddish purple tops and margins.

Potassium

- K — 19, 39
- 1-5%
- unique element - plants can accumulate in abundant amts - without exhibit - any toxicity symp.
  ↓
  Luxury consumption
- not a structural component
- regulatory role in plant metabolism

Why potassium improve the quality of food?

STCR & LEND
↳ Stomata ↳ Lodging
↳ Transport ↳ Enzy
↳ Crop qua ↳ Neutrali.
↳ Resist root ↳ Disease

Functions

- regulatory - regulates - opening / closing of stomata - photosy, H_2O & nutrient transport and plant cooling
- major role in transport of H_2O & nutrient - xylem
  def — NO_3^-, PO_4^{3-}, Ca^{2+}, Mg^{2+} and amino ā translo - hampered.
- ↑ root growth and ↑ drought tolerance
- neutralizes org. anions and other cmpds within plant - maintain cytoplasmic pH - 7-8 - ideal for many enzyme reactions.
- activates - enzymes (>60) - by exposing active reacⁿ sites.
  ↳ starch synthetase
  high K levels - starch moves from sites of prodⁿ to storage.
  ↳ nitrate - reductase
- Enhances crop quality - shelf life of fruits and veg.
- reduces lodging - ↑ winter hardiness.
- imparts disease resistance.

Def

- older leaves - chlorosis - leaf margins - f.b scorching and browning of tips
- progress inwards. - seeds and fruits shrivelled.
  - K deficiency - slow and stunted growth
  - lodge easily.

Calcium

Ca { 20 – 40

- Ca-sufficient — 0.2% – 1%
- most abundant in plant available forms in soil.
  - ↳ but defi – acid soils of tropics.

Func

- constituent of cell wall – Ca pectate – maintains integrity of mem.
- seeds – Ca-phytate
- imp. for growth of meristems and functioning of root tips
- protects root cells against ion imbalances, low pH, toxic ions (Al)
- neutralises charge on acidic mol. of phosphoric ā and organic ā — citric ā, malic ā, oxalic ā } injurious to plant growth.
- role in mitosis (cell division) – maintain chromosome structure
- activates phospholipase, arginine kinase, amylase, ATPase enzyme

GREN
- ↳ Growth
- ↳ Root
- ↳ Enzy
- ↳ Nutri

WSC
- ↳ Cell wall
- ↳ Seed
- ↳ Chromo.

Def

- < 0.1%
- seldom encountered – due abundance
- Ca-immobile in plant – def. sy. on younger structures.
- root system stunted
- young leaves – distorted, small, abnorm. green
- defi leaves – cup shaped, crinkled, terminal buds deteriorate
  - some breakdown of petioles.
- dessication of terminal buds
- weakening of stem stru.
- Blossom end rot – tomatoes
- Bitter pit – apples.

Magnesium

- Mg — 12, 24 — RuBP (Ribulose biphosphate carboxylase) — PEPC Phosphoenolpyruvate carboxylase — CO_2 fixation
- 0.1-0.4 %
- large part - Mg - ass. organic anions like malate (PEMA-P)
- Mg-const. of chlorophyll as Mg porphyrin with one Mg atom bound to 4 pyrrole rings. → Richard Willstatter. Without Mg, chl. can't capture sun energy

Functions

- photosynthesis
- activates enzymes — carbohydrate metabolism; nucleic a synthesis — ribo RuBisCo (PETE)
- promotes uptake and transl. of P and movem. of sugar within the plant
  - ATP - must be bound to Mg ion to - biolo. active.
  - essential const. of polyribosomes - key organelle in protein synthesis

Def.

- <0.1%
- interveinal chlorosis / streaked or patchy effects older lea.
- affected leaves - turn small, curve upwards at margin
- acute def. — leaves dry up - die
- Grass tetany - nutri. disorder - cattle grazing on Mg def. gr pastures well fertilized with K.

Sulphur

- S — 16, 32
- SO_4^{2-}
- some reports - foliage - SO_2
- 0.1% - 0.4% like P and Mg
- 4th major nutrient def. after N, P, K.

FAMGO — Ferredo, amino a, Glucos, oil, metabo

Function

- essen. comp. of amino a - cystine, cysteine, methionine.
- const. of ferredoxin containing nitrogenase - BNF & electron transfer reason.
- invol. in metabolic activities of vitamins, biotin, thiamine, coenzyme A
- invol. synthesis of glucosides in mustard oil — derivative of glucose
- ↑ oil quality in oilseed crops.

Def

- < 0.1-0.2%
- N:S - >16:1 - deficients (Plant N:S)
- younger growths - S immobile
- fading of green colour leaves - i.e chlorosis - most common
- most susceptible - Brassicas - lamina is restricted
  - leaves cupping - curling of leaf margins - arresting of growing points.
- older leaves - puckered with inward raised areas below veins.
  - ↳ orange or reddish tints - shed prematurely

Concept of Nutrient Availability

- Liebig's Law of Minimum - Principle developed by Carl Sprengel (1828) but later popularized by Justus Von Liebig
- nutrient present in least relative amount is the limiting nut
- extreme form: - even if all but one of the ess. elements are present, the absence of that one constituent renders crop barren
- Tandon and Kimmo (1993) - visualization - barrel having staves at diff. heights
- for a crop to produce to its full potential - all nutrients & factors of prodn - at sufficiency level. - nutrients neither def. nor toxic.

Mitscherlich's Law

- M. Law of physiological relationships -
  yield can be increased by in each single growth factor even when it is not present in minm as long as it is not pres. in optimum.
- M. growth law -
  increase in yield of a crop as a result of increasing a single growth fac. is ∝ to decrement from maxm yield obtainable by increasing that particular growth fac.

- plant growth ——→ follows — diminishing increment type of curve (yield curves)
- eqn — relatn betwn potential yield to amt of given nutrient —

$$\log(A-y) = \log A - cb$$

c — prop. constant
y — pot. yield when b amt of nut. present
A — pot. yield of crop when nut. is not deficient

- Percentage Yield Concept of Baule (1918)
- when > 1 nutrient is deficient, the final % sufficiency = product of indivi. sufficiency.

eg. If P — 80% of yield. (adeq. for)
K — 70% of yield

Final yield — $\frac{80}{100} \times \frac{70}{100}$ of yield.
$= \frac{56}{100}$ = 56% of yield. when both nutrients are adequate

Baule Unit
N – 223 – ninim
P – 145 – rose kgha⁻¹.
K – 76 – tub

Arthur Wallace
- Law of Maximum – Wallace and Wallace
- need when need is fully satisfied for every factor read in process, rate of process can be at its maxm potential, which is greater than sum of individual parts because of the sequentially additive interactions.

Bray's concept of Nutrient Avai
- Bray (1938) — fractions – variations in amounts – resp. for significant change in yield and response.
- availa. — not only on chem, physical prop. of soils.
 — ability of a plant to forage for them – root.

Bray's concept of Nutrient Mobility
- (Bray, 1954) — mobility – overall process – nutrients reach the sorbing root surfaces – thereby making possible their sorption into the plant.
- involves – soln or exchange of nutrient + movement to root surf.
- to Bray — mobile nut.
 — immobile nut.

- mobile :- not adsorbed by solid phase
  - remain in soln
  - carried to longer distances in response to their
  - & adsorption by plant roots
  - anions like nitrate, Cl^- or HCO_3^-

- immobile :- held on -ve charged surface of colloi. clays / om as ex. cations.
  - replace by and are in equilm with cations in soln
  - cations like Ca^{2+}, Mg^{2+}, K^+.

Concn of these cations - soln, controlled by

i) kind and amt of electrolytes in soil soln

ii) amt of diff. exch. cations present

iii) relative ease of release. (Bray, 1942)

P — held in soil —
- anion exchange
- ligand exchange
- adsorbed or precipt as sparingly soluble pho. of Fe, Al, Ca.

- Nutrient alone per se can't be mobile / immobile

↓

it is its form.

NO_3^- - mobile } soil.
NH_4^+ immobile }

- Plant

Mobile	Imm
N	B
P	Ca
K	Cu
Cl^-	Fe
Mg^-	Mn
Mo^-	Zn
	S

Soil

mob	Imm
H_3BO_3, $H_2BO_3^-$	NH_4^+
Cl^-	Ca^{2+}
NO_3^-,	Mg^{2+}
SO_4^{2-}	Cu^{2+}
	Fe^{2+}/Fe^{3+}
	MoO_4^{2-}
	$H_2PO_4^-$
	HPO_4^{2-}
	Ni^{2+}
	K^+

— Bray (1954) — ~~roo~~

root surface sorption zone

root system sorption zone

— mobile nutrients depend on total amt avail in soil (system sorp.)

— for immobile, total amt not imp — but imp in root surf-sorp zone and its possibility of transfer to plant root surface.

— Integrating these ideas
↓
Barber (1995)
↓
available / bio-available nutrient
(one — present in pool of ions in soil and — can move to plant root during growth if root close enough)
— one present in form — adsorbed by plants
— . . . in pool of nutrients — having effective diffusion coeff. $> 10^{-12}$ cm²/s

— Nielsen (1995) — bioavail. nut — one present in pool of avail. nutn — close enough to arrive at a nutrient & H_2O absorp root surface during period of say ten days.

— Avg. diffusion distance (Δx) =

$$\Delta x = \sqrt{2D_e t}$$

NKB CMP MZ MF

D_e = effective diff. coeff (cm²/s)
t = time (s) for which dispersion occurs.

NKB
CMP
MZ MF

Using these eqn.

Diffusing Ion	Diff. coef (D_e) at field cap (cm²/s)	Diff. time in 10 days (s)	Distance moved (cm)
			1.30
Nitrate	10^{-6}	8.64×10^5	0.40
K	10^{-7}		0.140
Borate	10^{-7}		0.13
Ca	10^{-8}		0.13
Mg	10^{-8}		0.04
Phosphate	10^{-9}		0.04
Mn	10^{-9}		0.04
Zn	10^{-9}		0.04
Molybdate	10^{-9}		0.013
Fe	10^{-10}		0.0013
for any ion to be avail	10^{-12}		

- Barber (1995) – avail. pool of nut – whose $De > 10^{-12}$ cm²/s.

For a nut. to be bio-avail – move a dist 0.0013 cm in 10 days.

$$\Delta x = \sqrt{2 \times 10^{-12} \times 10 \times 24 \times 60 \times 60} = 0.0013 \text{ cm}$$

used for quantification of soil volume capable of feeding the root and root radius for ~~ph~~ both mobile & imm.

eg. distance moved by NO_3^- — 1.3 cm.

H_2PO_4 — 0.04 cm.

Let density of soil (L_v) = 5 cm/cm³ of soil

avg. root radius = 0.01 cm.

In case of P — radial distance from centre of root → 0.05 cm [0.04 cm (diffusion dist + (radius) 0.01]

vol. of soil explored ~~by~~ for P by root

$$= L_v \cdot \pi r^2$$

$$= 5 \frac{cm}{cm^3} \times \pi \times (0.05 \text{ cm})^2$$

$$= 5 \times 3.14 \times (5 \times 10^{-2})^2 = 0.04 \text{ cm}^3/\text{cm}^3$$

$$= 4\%.$$

implies

i) 4% of soil vol. is explored for P

ii) 4% of avail P is bioavail over 10 days.

- can find out how much of root density sufficient to explore whole of soil vol. for NO_3^-

$$y \text{ (cm/cm}^3) \times 3.14 \times (1.31 \text{ cm})^2 = 1$$

$$\Rightarrow y = \frac{vol}{3.14} \times \frac{1}{(radius)^2} = \frac{vol}{\pi r^2}$$

$$= \frac{vol}{\pi r^2} \text{ cm/cm}^3.$$

Nutrient Movement in soil

- Movement
  - Diffusion (nutrients with H_2O mov. through H_2O)
  - Mass flow (with water)
  - root interception (plants roots - contact with soil - intercept the nutrients - contact exchange)

Mass flow

- movement — through soil - to root - in convective flow of H_2O — caused by plant water absorption.
- $J = V \times C_i$ — V → rate of H_2O flux into root; C_i - concn of ion in solution; J — rate of nut. transfer by mass flow
- avg. concn of Ca, K, P in soil soln of agri. soils.
  - Ca — 10^{-2}; K — 10^{-3} – 10^{-4}; P — 10^{-5} to 10^{-6} moles/litre.

eg. Total dry matter produced = 10 t/ha
= 10^4 kg/ha.

Amt of H_2O for prod. 1 kg of dry matter = 300 L.
for 10^4 kg = 3×10^6 L.

Concn of Ca in soln = 10^{-2} M/L
= $10^{-2} \times 40$ g/L
= 4×10^{-1} g/L

Amt of Ca moved with H_2O to plant root
= 3×10^6 L $\times 4 \times 10^{-1}$ g/L
= 1200 kg.
= 1200 kg/ha.

- actual — Ca crop - take up and translocate
  - Ca — 10-30 kg Ca/ha — importance of mass flow in supplying Ca.
  - K — 50-250 kg K/ha
  - P — 20-30 kg P/ha.
- Mass flow provides over abundance of Ca & Mg to plants. and for mobile nutrients

- Factors affecting Mass flow

- amount of H_2O ↘
- volume of soil – dry soil – no mass flow – no water to carry
- Temp – low temp reduces transpir. & evapor.

↓

↓ water flux.

- size of root system (but less critical)

Diffusion

- when mass flow unable to supply sufficient quantities of nut. but continued uptake occurs.

↓

concn of nutr. at root surface ↓

↓

concn gradient establish.

↓

Ions move by thermal (Brownian) motion from higher concn to ↓ concn.

- Movement of a nutrient ion – in response to concn gradient ↳ diffusion.

- amt of nut. ion ~~diff~~ diffused in unit area in unit time (F) – with concn gradient (dc/dx) – for steady-state diffusion

↓

Given by Fick's Law of diffusion.

$$F = -D.\frac{dc}{dx}$$

D – diff. co efficient (cm²/s)

↓ movement from ↑ to ↓ concn – opp to direction of concn gradient

- D – related to diff. soil parameters.

$D = D_w \cdot \theta \cdot f$ – Impedence factor related to continuity of diffusion path (dimensionless)

θ ↳ volumetric H_2O content (cm³/cm³)

D_w: coeff. in bulk H_2O (cm²/s)

- For transient state diffusion, change in concn with time at a fixed dist. x — Fick's 2nd law

$$\left(\frac{dc}{dt}\right) = D_e \left(\frac{d^2c}{dx^2}\right)$$

D_e → effective diff. coef (cm^2/s)

↓ for linear diffusion.

Factors aff. diffusion

- Eff. d. coeff. De

$$D_e = D_w \cdot \theta \cdot f \frac{1}{b} \quad \left[\because b = \frac{dc}{dc_1}\right]$$

b → Buffer power (dimensionless)

↳ slope of curve $= \frac{dc}{dc_1}$ — dc: change in concn of an ion in soil; dc_1: concn of same ion in solution.

- D_w – related to mobility of an ion.

$$D_w = \mu KT = \frac{KT}{6\pi r \eta}$$

μ = chemical mobility (cm/s)

K = Boltzman's constant

T = Temp (Kelvin)

η = visco.

r = radius of the ion.

So, factors which affect
- volumetric H_2O content
- Tortuosity
- buffer power

- Subs. the values

$$D_e = D_w \cdot \theta \cdot f \frac{1}{b}$$

$$= \mu KT \theta f \frac{1}{b}$$

$$= \frac{KT\theta f}{6\pi r \eta b}$$

- Distance travelled by nutrient ion (Δx) in cm/# — Einstein-Stokes' equation

$$\Delta x = \sqrt{2D_e t}$$

$$\Delta X = \sqrt{2\mu KT\theta f (1/b) t} = \sqrt{(KT\theta f t)/3\pi r \eta b}$$

Factors

- soil H_2O
- soil compaction
- temp
- chem. amendments

Soil water

- ↑ moist. content → ↑ diffusion coeff — until MC reaches saturation.
- In low MC — H_2O — thin film around soil part.
- For diffusion to occur — continuity of films is must.
- So, ↑ rise in H_2O content — makes less viscous, water films grows — ↑ De values.

Soil compaction

- vol. basis
  - soil solid 50%
  - liquid 15-35%
  - gaseous 15-35%
- Incremental ↑ in soil compaction at same MC — exclusion of air
  ↓
  soil part. come closer
  ↓
  continuity of moisture flows ↑.
  ↓
  path to traversed by ion by diffusion less tortuous
  ↓
  De increases.
  ↓
  increases to maxm at a sp. level of soil compaction - critical bulk density (ρ_c)
  → At ρ_c - whole air is excluded - only solid + liquid.
  ↓
  Above ρ_c — De exhibits ↓ trend with ↑ ρ_c.
  ↳ exclude H_2O — reduces De value.
- Moisture and BD interact — influence De — by creating variation in path length — tortuosity / impedence (f)

LE

Temp

- General rule

Rate of chem. reacn – doubles – for every 10°C ↑. (Van Hoff's Rule)

- ↑ temp – ↑ D..

$D_w = \nu kT = \frac{KT}{6\pi\eta}$

- Low temp – diffusion virtually ceases –.

↓

Reason – ions need minm activation energy for making them participate in chem. reacn.

- Rising temp – overcome this activ. energy.

↓

↑ fluidity

↓

↓ viscosity

↓

↑ Diffusion.

Chemical amendments

- Buffer power $b = \frac{dC}{dC_1}$ – soil / – soln

- amendments (lime – acid soils / gypsum – sodic) / (manures & fert, chelating agents)

↓

modify concn of nut. ions in soln.

↓

b values changes as a result of change of C_1 & C values.

- Liming – raises pH of acid soils

↓

concn of cations ↓.

an anions ↑. in soil solution

↓

D of cations ↓

D of anions ↑

$(Zn^{2+}) = 10^{5.8}(H^+)^2$

$(Cu^{2+}) = 10^{2.8}(H^+)^2$

$(Fe^{3+}) = 10^{2.2}(H^+)^3$

$(MoO_4^{2-}) = 10^{-20.4}(H^+)^{2-}$

App of gypsum – reduces pH so. De rises

OM – low molc. organic subst

↓

forms complexes.

↓

↑ in concn of metals in soln

↓ b → ↑ De. ←

Root Interception

- Jenny and Overstreet (1939)
  - ↳ Theories of cation exchange.
  - ↓ mechanism for reacn between adsorbents or solids – without partici. of free electrolytes
- Theories of contact exchange – concept of overlapping oscillation spaces of adsorbed ions, or redistribution within intermingling electric double layers.

[Clay] – M^+ + H^+ [Root] → [Clay] – H^+ + M^+ [Root]

and modelled as

[Clay] [M^+] [Root]
[H^+]

- On further refining – concept of root interception
  - ↓ Stanley A. Barber of Purdue State Univ, USA
- soil nut. don't need to move to surface but root itself must approach.
- quantity of nut by root int = ~~qua quantity~~ root volume i.e.
  - ↓ generally, < 1% of soil volume in 0–20 cm depth
  - ↓ hence.
- can be enhanced by mycorrhizae.

- Relative Imp of M.F and Diff
- When mass flow is – unable to meet the demand of plant – diffusion sets in – concn gradient develop.
- Diffusion vol :– vol. of soil – concn of nut. ~~at a con~~ is lower than bulk of soil soln – due to absorption by plant root
- ↳ determined by diff. charact.

Diffusion vol = {~~Db Δc~~

Diff. volume =

$$\left\{\left[\frac{D}{b}\, \delta C\, \frac{t}{Q}\, (Ar + Rr)\right]^2 - (Rr)^2\right\} \cdot \frac{1}{(Rr)^2}$$

D = Diff. coeff.

b = buffer power

δC = concn gradient

Q = amt of nut. taken up in time t

t = time - diff. occurs

Ar = surface area of 1 g of root

Rr = radius of the root

- Diffusion moves nutrients — slowly — 10 days NO_3 → 1.3 cm, Fe — 0.03 cm.
- So, to traverse larger distances, movement ↓ Mass flow or convective flow.
- Once mass flow delivers nut — in diff. volume — water needn't reach the root surface.
  So, ↳ mass flow - special imp — in charging the diff. volume.
- Diffusion — sp. imp — in rhizosphere.
  Mass flow and diff — so — complementary — both can be rate limiting but not at same time.

Nutrient uptake by Plants

- nutrient uptake depends on — plant's need; soil's ability to supply.
- — absorption of nut; nutrient uptake.

Absorption of nut

- absorbed in ionic form.
- rel. between ion concn (C) and rate of uptake (I)

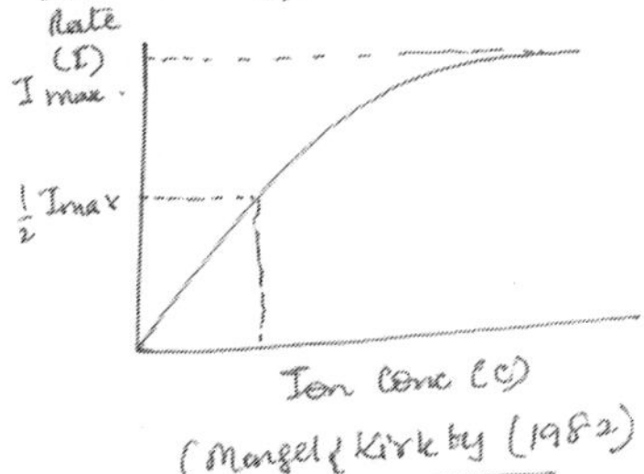

(Mengel & Kirkby (1982))

- increases curvilinearly with ↑ in ion concn in soil soln at root surface

$$I_n = \frac{I_{max} \times C_{la}}{K_m + C_{la}}$$

I_n — Rate of Ion uptake

I_{max} — Max^m rate of ion uptake when conc^n C_{la} is not limiting

C_{la} — conc^n of nut. in soil sol^n at root surface

K_m — Michaelis - Menten constant = conc^n of nut. ion in soil sol^n when $I_n = I_{max}/2$

Leonor Michael
Maud Menten

↓ reduces to following linear forms.

$$\frac{1}{I_n} = \left(\frac{1}{I_{max}}\right) + \left(\frac{K_m}{I_{max}}\right) \times \left(\frac{1}{C_{la}}\right)$$

→ equation known as Lineweaver - Burke plot

and

$$I_n = I_{max} - \left[K_m \times \frac{I_n}{C_{la}}\right]$$

→ Eadie - Hofstee plot

(used to charac. & compute absorption parameters I_{max} and K_m)

- & Min^m conc^n of nut ion in soil solution (C_{min}) below which plant roots - unable to take up ion -

$$I_n = \frac{I_{max} \times [C_{la} - C_{min}]}{K_m + (C_{la} - C_{min})}$$

(modified from previous eqn)

Nature of Ion absorption

- To know nature of ion absorption - roots - necessary to know electrochemical potential (μ) of an ion, j.

$$\mu_j = \mu_j^0 + RT \ln a_j + z_j FE$$

μ_j^0 ↳ Standard el. ch potential of ion j

R ↳ Universal Gas constant = $8.314\ JK^{-1} mol^{-1}$

T = Temp (K)

a_j = activity of ion j in sol^n

z_j = valency of ion j.

F = Faraday's constant = $9.6 \times 10^4\ C\ mol^{-1}$

E = Electrical potential

– Driving force for movement of an ion in direction x – obtained by differentiation – wrt x

$$\frac{d\mu_j}{dx} = \frac{RT}{a_j} \times \frac{da_j}{dx} + z_j F\left(\frac{dE}{dx}\right)$$

(first term: concn gradient; second term: electrical gradient)

So, ion moves in response to concn gradient & elec. gradient.

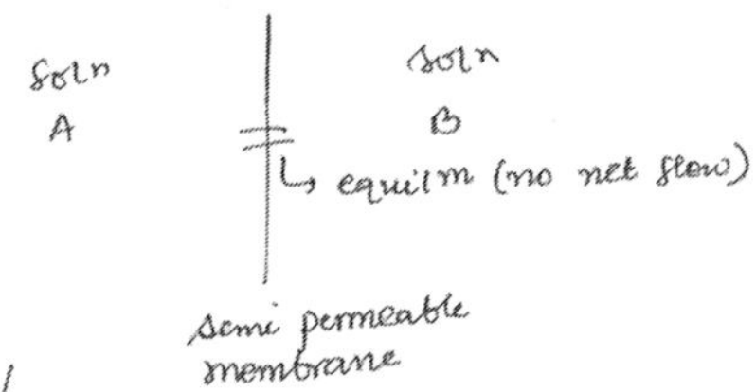

under this concn – $\frac{d\mu_j}{dx} = 0$ so,

$$0 = \frac{RT}{a_j} \times \frac{da_j}{dx} + z_j F\left(\frac{dE}{dx}\right)$$

$$\Rightarrow z_j F\left(\frac{dE}{dx}\right) = -\left(\frac{RT}{a_j}\right)\left(\frac{da_j}{dx}\right)$$

$$\Rightarrow \frac{dE}{dx} = -\frac{RT}{z_j F}\left(\frac{1}{a_j}\right)\left(\frac{da_j}{dx}\right)$$

– If plant cell immersed into a soln (with membrane) – portion of soln – enters the membrane / outside.

– so, elec. potentials of inside $[E_i]$ / outside $[E_o]$ soln –

$$E^i = -\frac{RT}{z_j F} \ln a_j^i$$

$$E^o = -\frac{RT}{z_j F} \ln a_j^o$$

Difference between these pot = Nernst potential, E^N

$$E^N = E^i - E^o$$

$$= \frac{RT}{z_j F}\left(\ln a_j^o - \ln a_j^i\right)$$

$$= \frac{RT}{z_j F} \ln \frac{a_j^o}{a_j^i}$$

$$E^N = \frac{RT}{z_j F} \ln \frac{a_j^o}{a_j^i}$$

– for univalent cation like K^+, if activity outside = 1.0 mM/L
inside = 10 mM/L

$$E^N = \frac{2.303\ RT}{(+1)F} \cdot \log\left(\frac{1}{10}\right) = -59.2\,mV.$$

Similarly for univalent anion like Cl^-

$$E^N = \frac{\quad}{(-1)} \quad = +59.2\,mV$$

– Root membranes ⇒ electr. p.d = –120 mV to –180 mV
↓
can hold higher concn of cations – cytoplasm relative to outside
– But not anions.
So, that's why – at normal cation concn – cations absorbed in response to electrochemical pot. gradient.
– pumping of anions inside – against the electro pot. gradient
eg. Membrane with –120 mV – can accumulate 100 times more univalent
10000 times dival.
1,000,000 triva
inside the cell compared to outside.

– Thermodynamically,
absorption – ions – plant roots – along elec. pot. gradient = passive absorption.
. . . . – against " – . . . . by expenditure of metabolic energy = active absorption

Active and Passive absorption

– can predict active/passive – by knowing concn of ions in
– apoplasm (outside)
– cytoplasm (inside)
– also electrical potential (Em) of membrane.

If E_{cal} = Nernst ~~ele~~ pot.

driving force (E_d)

$E_d = E_m - E_{cal}$

- For cations → –ve value of E_d → passive uptake.
  +ve value → active uptake.

→ For anions → opposite.

Nutrient Interaction in Plant

- crop yield = result – simultaneous growth factors.
- all effects of various factors – common – all based on same (principle of nutrient uptake – 'General Relation'
  → but partly differ – as they are of diff. functions.
- General Relation for growth function (based on diff. eqn)

~~$\frac{1-q}{\theta}\left(\frac{1-q}{\theta}\right)\left[1-\frac{q}{a}(x-x_0)\right]\left[1-\frac{q}{b}(y-y_0)\right]=F$~~

$$\left[1-\frac{q}{\theta}\right]\left[1-\frac{q}{a(x-x_0)}\right]\left[1-\frac{q}{b(y-y_0)}\right]=F$$

q = actual yield

θ = maxm yield

q_x = ~~~~ theore. yields of x

q_y " " "

a . b = growth parameter

F = flexibility factor

$q_x = a(x-x_0)$

$q_y = b(y-y_0)$

$$=\left(1-\frac{q}{\theta}\right)\left(1-q/q_x\right)\left(1-q/q_y\right)=F$$

Flexibility factor – range of ratios of nut. absorbed without which unhampered growth is not possible.

If ratio - fixed – then F = 0

vary = small +ve value of F.

Ion Pumps and ATPases

- ATPase — group of enzymes — located on plant cell membrane
  - ↳ split ATP → ADP and P_i with energy

$$ATP \rightarrow ADP + P_i + \text{Energy}$$

↓ used for operation of H^+ pumps and consequential ion transport

- Plant membrane ATPase — ~~cell me~~ plasma membrane & tonoplast
  - ↳ central component in Mitchell's electro-osmotic theory (based on operation of ion pumps)
- ATPase run H^+ pump.

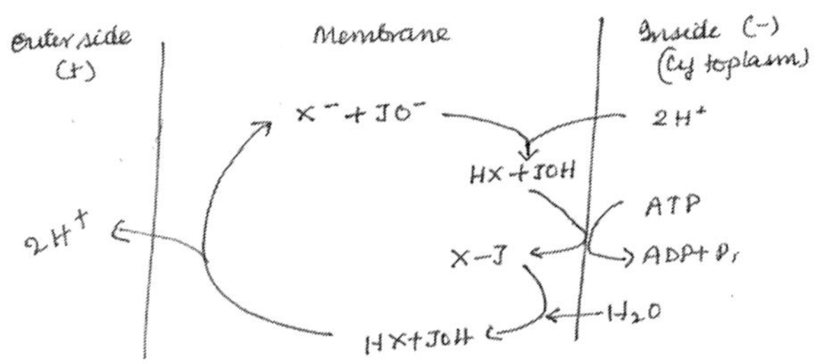

- Mengel & Kirkby (1982)
- i) - membrane mobile anions X^-, JO^- + $2H^+$ of cytoplasm → protonated - HX and JOH

↓

ii) HX and JOH induce breakdown of ATP → ADP, P_i, energy and process get condensed into X-J complex.

↓ complex undergo hydrolysis → XH and JOH

↓ using energy of splitting ATP ← $2H^+$ move to outer side of membrane ← deprotonated as X^- and JO^-

↓ eject 2 protons (H^+) out of cell → cycle repeated continuously

↓ responsible for −ve charge of cell and alkaline reac^n of cytoplasm.

– ATPase H^+ pumps – works on potential (chemical and electrical) with driving force given below:

$$pmf = \Delta pH + \psi$$

pmf = proton motive force / elect chem. pot. gradient of H^+ ions across the membrane.

ΔpH = change in pH in cytopl. and apoplasm

ψ = electrical pot. diff. across memb.

→ force by which protons transported – against an electroch. gradient across the membrane

so, efflux of protons out of cytoplasm

↓

energy-requiring process

– ATPase H^+ Pumps = located on plasmalemma and tonoplast

↳ control pH of

- cytoplasm = 7.3–7.6
- vacuole = 4.5–5.9
- apoplasm = 5.5

Variations in pH and elect. pot. diff. acro induce secondary reacn in terms of movement of cations and anions into cytoplasm and vacuoles.

– Cations – transported passively or downhill across the plasmalemma into cytoplasm along elec. pot. gradient of –120 mV to –180 mV.

↳ So called uniport transport.

– If concn of K^+ in apoplasm = 1 mM/L → concn of K^+ in cytoplasm = 100 mM/L (in equiln)

If K^+ concn < 1 mM/L → K^+ will still be taken up but at expense of energy.

↳ Counter transport

- can also accompany H^+ when H^+ is moving back to cytoplasm – in response of to H^+ gradient — co-transport
- co-transport of anions along with proton influx across plasmalemma

↓

distinct possibility

↓

referred as co-transport or symport

- Cations →

Carrier hypothesis

- Epstein (1953).
- describe active accumuln of ions across cell membrane
- carrier molecules exist on semi-perm. cell membrane
  - ↳ so called because - possess specific binding sites for ions. part.
- ions transported combine - carrier molecules – ion-carrier complex

↓

Pass through semi-permeable membrane (allows selective diffusion)

- Ion uptake involving carrier mol – Mengel & Kirkby (1982)

Ion + carrier ← say phosphorylated compound

↓

Ion-carrier complex

↓

preferential diffusing across membrane

↓

encounters phosphatase ensyme

↓

splits off Phosphate from complex

↓

carrier loses its affinity for ion

↓

ion released in cytoplasm

↓

regeneration of released carrier and activation by phosphokinase (on inner side of boundary) — by utilization of energy released from breakd. of ATP

↓

activated carrier again traverses to outer side of plasma membrane

↓

intercepts an ion → transports across plasma memb. → cycle loses its cytoplasm.

(Cycle goes on — Chemically pictured by Mengel and Kirkby (1982))

– Carr. hypo. described by enzyme kinetics — known as Michaelis-Menten kinetic

$$I_n = \frac{I_{max} \times C_{la}}{K_m + C_{la}}$$

– Ion uptake described by two constants. I_{max} & K_m evaluated by using either :—

$$\frac{1}{I_n} = \left(\frac{1}{I_{max}}\right) + \left(\frac{K_m}{I_{max}}\right) \times \left(\frac{1}{C_{la}}\right)$$ – Lindweaver Burkee plot

$$I_n = I_{max} - \left[K_m \times \frac{I_n}{C_{la}}\right]$$ – Eadie-Hofstee's plot

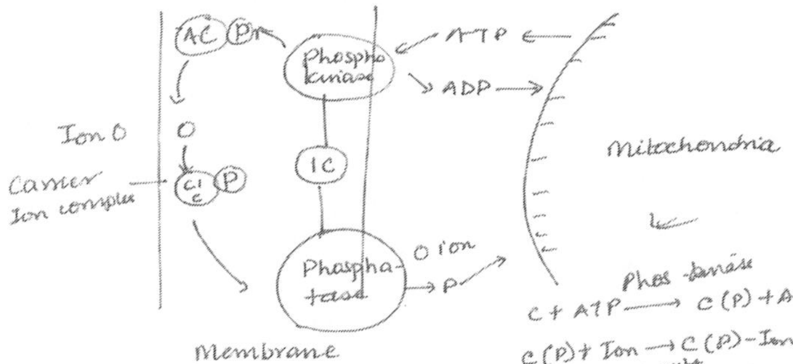

$$C + ATP \xrightarrow{\text{Phos-kinase}} C(P) + ADP$$

$$C(P) + Ion \rightarrow C(P)\text{-}Ion$$

$$C(P)\text{-}Ion \xrightarrow{\text{Phosphatase}} Carrier + P_i + Ion$$

$$\text{Net: } Ion + ATP \rightarrow Ion + ADP + P_i$$

Uptake of Nutrients by Crops

– Uptake need not be same as it occur in soil

eg. Ca most abundant in soil.

But uptake of Ca in wheat — much less than those of N, P, K.

– Consumption of the produce — removes nutrients
– Intensive agriculture — nutrient depletion
– So, information on nutrient uptake necessary :—

Major nut	Total uptake (kg/ha)	Micro	(bdd – sridd)
N	30 – 180 (md – lgd)	Fe	600 – 4400
P	4 – 43 (r – sum)	Mn	17 – 1857 (lt – lgst)
K	30 – 200 (md – ndd)	Zn	28 – 725 (ng – tns)
Ca	15 – 114 (ls – lls)	Cu	12 – 639 (ln – bmq)
Mg	4 – 55 (n – ss)	B	65 – 342 (bs – mnt)
S	5 – 33 (s – mm)	Mo	11 – 45 (ll – ns)

Generalizations:

- Uptake of N = Uptake of K
- Ca uptake = $\frac{1}{2}$ of N and K.
- Uptake of P, Mg, S = similar = $\frac{1}{5}$ th of N or K.
- Fe uptake = 100 of N/K
- Mn, Zn, B uptake = $\frac{1}{2}$ Fe = 2 Cu = 200 of N and K = $\frac{1}{40}$ of P, Mg, S
- Cu uptake = $\frac{1}{2}$ Zn, B, Mn | Mn, Zn, B.
- Mo uptake = $\frac{1}{10}$ of Zn.

If Mo uptake = 1,

Cu = 5
Mn, Zn, B = 10
Fe = 20
P, Mg, S = 400
Ca = 1000
N, K = 2000 units

N – mad – lagd
P – r – rim
K – mad – nadd
Ca – ls – llr – (lose-lubry)
Mg – r – riss
S – 8 – mm
Fe – badd – rrdd
Mn – late – lagst
Zn – nag – tons
Cu – lone – beamq
B – bis – mast
Mo – ll – rs. (lot – rose)

$N = K = 2Ca = 5 PMgS = \frac{1}{100}$ Fe Cu $= \frac{1}{200}$ Mn Zn B $= \frac{1}{20}$ Mo

Factors affecting uptake

- Types of crops (1) and cropping systems (11)
  - Cereal crops
  - Pulses and Oilseed
  - Root, Fruit, Forage. Plantation
  - Cropping System
  - Fert app. rates
- ~~Fert app rates~~.
- Conjunctive app of (26) organic Manures + Inorg. Fert.

Types of crops and cropping systems

- Cereal crops
  - finger millet – maxm uptake
  - maize – least uptake.
- Rice = wheat (in consuming quantities of N)
- In case of K = almost equal but consumption < in wheat.
- P and micronutrients (except Zn) → > in rice crop. Reason: higher mobilization of the nutrients
- Higher cons. of S and Zn by upland crops — ass. with higher avail. under oxidative envn.

- In acid soils — nutrient removal of wheat - low.
- Uptake of B and Mo — low in highly leached acid soils.

Pulses and oilseed crops
(N) (K)

- produce lower economic yields than cereals.
- Uptake of N higher — legumes.
  Uptake of K higher — oilseed.
  much comes from BNF
- Uptake of Ca, S — oilseed — high
- In mustard and raya - uptake of S > up. of P.
- On basis of S uptake (relative to N): —

  yellow mustard = taramira > raya > sesamum > soybean = sunflower > groundnut = mungbean = black gram = pigeon pea. > linseed > gram = lentil

- S-uptake more in oilseed (except linseed)
- Soybean (legume and oilseed) - removes more N, P, K, Ca, Mg, S.
- Generally, cereals 1-6 kg S/t
  pulses require 5-13 kg S/t of economic produce with mean values 4 / 8 / 12 kg S/t
  oilseed 5-20 kg S/t

Roots, Fruits, Plantat, Forages

- Forages = more drymatter production — removes more N, P, K.
- K - more by fruit, root, plantation.

Cropping Systems

- de function — total dry matter prodn
  — nature of crops
  — soil fertility.

- System with ↑ dry matter - removes more.
- rice based → rice - wheat - exhaustive than rice-rice

fert appln rate ✓

- uptake function — { nutrient cont. in plant / drymatter production } both ↑ with ↑ fert app rate

- it also catalyze removal of other nutrients

conjunctive use

- Sustainable productivity
- liming — Mo avail ↑.
- provide secondary nut.

—★—

Active Transport

(i) against elec. gradient
(ii) requires celular energy
(iii) endocytosis, cell membrane & Na-K pump
(iv) - Transport mol. through cell membrane against.
(v) disrupts eqn.
(vi) 9as, large cells
(vii) sugars, amino a need to enter cells by protein pump - active transport

Passive

- along — Defn
- doesn't require. — Energy req
- Diffusion, Osmosis — Type of transp.
- maintains dynam eqn of between cells and extracellular fluid. — Functions.
- no net diffussion.
- anything soluble in lipids, small monochor. — Type of Part.
- maintains eqn of cells — Imp.

Mineral Nutrition

- 119 elements
- nutrient – complete life cycle
- deficient – low – severely limits growth – def. symptoms
- Insufficient – low – growth reductions – but not def. symp.
- sufficient – optimum range
- toxic : too high.
- Available Nutrient :–

Nitrogen

- amino ā. proteins, nucleic ā, purines and pyrimidines.
- nucle. a – RNA
  DNA
- quality of leafy vegetables and fodder.
- protein quality of foodgrain

↑ glutamic ā. proline, phenylalanine, cystine, methionine, tyrosin and

↓ lysine, histidine, arginine, aspartic ā, threonine, glycine, valine, leucin.

- Deficiency :– stunted growth
  – chlorosis (older leaves)
    ↳ proteolysis.
  – reductn in flowering

739
P – 2.29
Mg – 1.7 – 0.6
Ca – 0.8

KNO_3 – N (13)
DAP – N (18), P (46)
KCl – K_2O (60)

OM – N (5), P (0.5), S (0.5)
SSP – Ca (18-21%), S (12), P_2O_5 (16).
TSP – Ca (48-52), P_2O_5 (12-14), S (1-1.5)
$Ca(NO_3)_2$ – Ca (19), N (15)
MgO – Mg (55).
Basic slag – Mg (3-4), P_2O_5 (3-8), Ca (20).
Serpentine – Mg (26)
$Mg(NO_3)_2$ – Mg (16)
Ca-EDTA – Ca (3-5)
Mg-EDTA – Mg (2-4)
$MgCl_2.10H_2O$ – Mg (8-9)
C:N – 20, 30 : 1
N → 1.5 – 1.7
C:P – 200, 300 : 1
P – 0.3 – 0.2
C:S – 200, 300 : 1
S – 0.15 – 0.22
$(NH_4)_2S_2O_3$ – N (12), S (26)
K_2SO_4 – S (19)
Gypsum – S (21), Ca (30)
$(NH_4)_2(SO_4)_2$ – S (21)
CAN – Ca (8)
$CaCN_2$ – N (21), Ca (40)

$NaNO_3$ – N (16)
$NH_4 \cdot (PO_4)_3$ – N (11-13), P_2O_5 (48-62)
Urea AP – N (21-38); SO_4 (13-42)
Urea SO_4 – N (30-40), SO_4 (6-11)
Urea formal – N (38)
SCU – S (38)
Thiourea – 37
Nit. oxamide – 32
IBDU – 32
Urea Z – 33-38
Kieserite – Mg (27)
Epsomite – Mg (16)
Raw bone meal – N (3-5)
RP – Citrate P_2O_5 (5-17)

Soil Classification

- grouping of objects — orderly — logical
- differentiating characters.
- lower category (soil series) — more no. of diff. charact.
- higher cat. (soil order) — lesser.
- within each class — central concept / nucleus / idealized individual
  - typifies the class
  - individual members are related.

Purposes of soil classif.

- Organise knowledge — economy of thoughts
- recognize properties of objects
- learn new relationships and principle — population
- Establish groups or subdivisions — for practical and applied purposes —
  - predicting their behaviour
  - identifying their potential uses
  - estimate productivity
  - transfer agro tech. from research farms to cult. fields.

Evolution of Soil Classif. Systems

- Early systems
  - ↳ aim was utilitarian (5)
  - ↳ economic (taxation) . physical (texture) , chemical (acidic) etc . geological (parent mat) , physiographic (landscape)

Dokuchaiev's Genetic System

Order	Sub-order	Great soil groups
Zonal Soils	(6)	vary
	cold zone	Tundra
	arid zone (light colour)	Seirozem Brown Reddish Brown (5) Desert Red desert
	semi arid, subhumid, humid (dark colour)	Chestnut Redd. chestnut (5) Chernozem Prairie or Brunizem Reddish Prairie

- forest grassland transition — degraded chernozem, noncalcic brown
- podzolized soils of timbered regions — Podzol; Gray wooded/Gray podzolic; Brown podz.; soil - brun acide; Gray brown pod.; red yellow pod. (6)
- Laterite soils - warm temper and tropical region — Redd - brown lateritic; Yell - brown Lat.; Laterite (3)

Intrazonal

(3)

- Halomorphic (saline and alkali) arid and littoral deposits — Solonchak (saline); solonetz (partly leach. solonchak); Soloth
- Hydromorphic (marshes, swamps) — Humic gley; Low humid gley; Planosols; Groundwater podzol; " laterite; Alpine Meadow Soils; Bog and Half bog
- Calcimorphic — Brown forest soil; Rendzina

Azonal

No suborder — Lithosols; Regosols; Alluvial.

ENDOPEDONS KONGSAPCDF — NAKOSCG

Argillic horizon

- silicate clay enriched
- illuviation of clay → by percolating H_2O and deposited as clay skins or cutans on ped faces and walls of the pores.
- B-horizon atleast 1.2 times as much clay content from above or 3% more clay cont. if eluvial (bleached) layer has < 15% clay
- or 8% more clay
  > 40% clay
- atleast 1/10 th of all overlying horizons or more than 15cm thick.

- Natric horizon
  - high Na^+ clay enriched
  - columnar or prismatic structure
  - all reqd. of argillic
  - but 15% or more of EC (exchange complex) saturated with Na^+ or more exch. Mg^{2+} + Na^+ than Ca^{2+} + exchange acidity at pH 8.2.

→ Agric horizon (CSH)
  - illuviation of clay, silt and humus – directly under plough sole/layer – due to long and continuous cultivation

- Spodic horizon
  - humus and/or sesquioxide enrich – with/without Fe.
  - cold humid regions.
  - 85% of > of spodic materials in 2.5 cm or more thick that is not a part of any Ap-horizon.
  - rare in India.
  - Podsols – Himalayas – but don't meet requirements.

- Sombric horizon
  - free draining
  - located not under an albic horizon
  - colour (darkness) and base status like umbric.
    ↓ (colour) Values ≤ 3.0 (moist), > 5.0 (dry), chroma < 3.5 (moist)
    ↓ (base status) < 50% (BS)

(mollic)

- illuvⁿ of humus and not of Al / Na

Cambic horizon

- colour or structural B-horizon
- alteration by - physical movement or
  - chemical weathering. } → pedogenic process ↓ alter the material ↓ to form soil structure liberate free iron oxides to form ↓ silicate clays.

← obliterate most evidences of original rock structure in more than 50% of volume

↓

But alteration - not enough to destroy volcanic glass, allophane, glass, feldspars and micas.

↓

And similarly, illuviation of oxides, humus or clay — must not be enough — qualify for argillic, spodic ho.

- horizon extremely variable in mineralogy — due to pedogenic youthfulness — wide envn condi.

Kandic horizon

- low activity clays with/ord clay-skins.
- CEC of < 16 cmol (p⁺) kg⁻¹ soil at pH 7.
- ECEC of ≤ 12 cmol (p⁺) . . . .
- clay content ↑ at upper boundary of > 1.2 × clay within a vertical distance of < 15 cm → abrupt but clear textural boundary
- no stratification.

Oxic horizon

- Fe/Al oxides enriched
- dominance of 1:1 clay
- silica ↓ leached